FRUIT OF THE WOMB

Parenting with Purpose from Seed to Harvest

DR. ELSWORTH NEALE

FRUIT OF THE WOMB

Fruit of the Womb: Parenting with Purpose from Seed to Harvest © 2025 Dr. Elsworth Neale. All rights reserved.

No part of this book may be reproduced or transmitted in any form without prior written permission from the author, except for brief quotations in reviews or articles.

Scripture quotations, unless otherwise noted, are from the **Holy Bible, New International Version® (NIV)**, © 1973–2011 by Biblica, Inc.™ Used by permission.

Verses marked **KJV** are from the public domain *King James Version*; **NLT** from the *New Living Translation*, © 1996–2015 by Tyndale House Foundation; **AMP** from the *Amplified Bible*, © 2015 by The Lockman Foundation; and **MSG** from *The Message*, © 1993–2018 by Eugene H. Peterson. All used by permission.

Published by **Kingdom Lifestyle Publishers**, Brooklyn, New York, USA

Printed in the United States of America

ISBN: 979-8-9937201-0-4

Cover Design: Mr. Lester Ifill

Visit: www.drels.org

DEDICATION

To every parent who has ever prayed over a crib, wiped away tears in the dark of night, or whispered blessings over a sleeping child, this book is for you.

To the mothers who carry *seeds of promise* in their wombs, and the fathers who guard *orchards of destiny* in their homes, may you never forget that parenting is *holy ground*.

I dedicate this work to my own children *Juel, Yohance,* and *Juda,* who have taught me more about God's love than I could ever have imagined. You are my sweetest fruit, my living reminders that the *heritage of the Lord* is indeed a reward.

And above all, I dedicate this book to the *Lord of the Harvest,* who entrusts us with seeds and calls us to cultivate them with purpose. May every page bring Him glory.

FOREWORD

As the author of an award-winning book on raising godly children, I am deeply concerned about the growing challenges and the accompanying apathy associated with parenting in this modern era. In a time when distraction, cultural shifts, and competing ideologies seem to erode the foundations of family life, the task of raising children with purpose, love, and godly direction has never been more urgent.

This book, so brilliantly written with its colorful metaphors and vivid illustrations, puts parenting back into its proper perspective. While it emphasizes the weight of parental responsibility, it also beautifully expands on the joy of nurturing these precious gifts from God. It represents not only a valuable addition to the existing body of knowledge available to parents but also a unique work crafted to highlight the delight, wonder, and fulfillment that flow from the sacred calling of parenthood.

Using the distinctive characteristics of different fruits, *Dr. Neale* skillfully reminds us of the unique personality and God-given potential within every child. Just as no two fruits are identical in flavor, texture, or purpose, no two children are the same in temperament, gifting, or destiny. Each child is a special gift from

God, infused with divine purpose and unlimited possibilities to impact the world for good.

This is more than a parenting guide. It is a gentle but powerful reminder that children are not merely to be managed, but to be celebrated, cultivated, and released to flourish. With wisdom that is both practical and inspiring, *Dr. Neale* calls parents back to the joy of raising children, not as a burdensome duty but as a sacred privilege.

I wholeheartedly commend this book to every parent, grandparent, guardian, or caregiver who longs to see the next generation rise in strength, beauty, and purpose.

Rev. Dr. Paul Carrette

Senior Pastor

Church of Living Waters, Oxon Hill, Maryland

ACKNOWLEDGMENTS

Books are never written alone. They are watered by encouragement, cultivated by wisdom shared, and harvested through the faithful prayers of others.

I wish to thank my family, who gave me space and strength to write. To my children, thank you for allowing me to learn from your laughter, your tears, and your questions. You have been my *living classroom,* and this book is as much yours as it is mine.

I am deeply grateful to my spiritual father, mentors, colleagues, and fellow laborers in ministry who affirmed this vision and reminded me that the work of parenting is both *sacred* and *urgent.* Your examples of faithfulness continue to inspire me.

To my church family, who have walked with me through the seasons of life, thank you for embodying *community,* the cluster where children truly thrive.

Finally, to every reader of this book, thank you for trusting me to speak into your parenting journey. May the wisdom of *God's orchard* encourage you, challenge you, and equip you to raise children who will *bear fruit that remains*.

PREFACE

When I first sensed the stirring to write this book, it wasn't to add another title to the many parenting resources already available. It came from a deeper conviction that God was calling me to speak to parents not only as a teacher but as a fellow traveler, a shepherd, and a father.

Over the years, I have seen the immeasurable gift that children are, and the sacred weight that comes with raising them. Parenting is one of life's greatest joys, but also one of its greatest responsibilities. The Bible calls children a *heritage of the Lord*—His reward, His treasure, His seed entrusted to us. That truth has shaped how I have raised my own children and how I have walked alongside countless families in ministry.

The Lord drew me again and again to the imagery of *fruit*. In Scripture, fruit is never just fruit; it is evidence of growth, character, and legacy. Jesus said that we would be known by our fruit. As I prayed and reflected, I began to see children through that same divine lens as fruit in God's orchard, each carrying unique qualities and lessons about growth, resilience, tenderness, and balance.

That vision became *Fruit of the Womb: Parenting with Purpose from Seed to Harvest*. This is not a manual of formulas or quick fixes;

parenting is far too holy and complex for that. Instead, it is a collection of reflections rooted in Scripture and illustrated by creation, calling us back to intentional, Spirit-led cultivation. Each chapter draws lessons from the characteristics of fruit, the apple, banana, grape, coconut, lemon, pear, and more, to reveal truths about children and to guide parents in nurturing them toward wholeness and fruitfulness.

I wrote this book with three burdens on my heart:

• To remind parents that children are not accidents but *assignments,* divine gifts entrusted with purpose and destiny.

• To encourage weary and overwhelmed parents that even the *sour seasons* are part of God's plan to build strength and resilience.

• To call parents to *a generational vision,* recognizing that our children are not only fruit for today but seeds for tomorrow.

My prayer is that as you journey through these pages, you will see your children with fresh eyes, celebrating their uniqueness, enduring their challenges, and embracing your role as a cultivator in God's orchard. May you be strengthened by His Word, encouraged by these reflections, and empowered by the Holy Spirit to raise a generation that glorifies Him.

I do not write as one who has mastered parenting, but as one who has learned through both mistakes and mercies. I hope that these reflections, anchored in Scripture and grace, will serve as tools for your journey.

May this book remind you that parenting is not a burden to endure but a calling to embrace, a sacred partnership with God in cultivating lives that bear eternal fruit.

And may the *fruit of your womb,* your sons and daughters, grow into men and women whose lives are sweet, resilient, whole, and fruitful for generations to come.

With gratitude to God and love for you, the reader,

Dr. Elsworth Neale

FRUIT OF THE WOMB

CONTENTS

Dedication iv

Foreword IV

Acknowledgments VI

Preface VII

Introduction XI

Chapter 1: The Apple — Sweetness And Innocence 1

Chapter 2: The Mango: Richness Of Destiny 14

Chapter 3: The Banana: Growth In Clusters 27

Chapter 4: The Grapes: Connectedness And Legacy 40

Chapter 5: The Watermelon: Hidden Riches Within 55

Chapter 6: The Cherry – Small But Precious 69

Chapter 7: The Pineapple: Strength And Sweetness 85

Chapter 8: The Orange: Wholeness And Healing 99

Chapter 9: The Strawberry: Tenderness & Growth In Low Places 114

Chapter 10: The Coconut: Layers Of Discovery 129

Chapter 11: The Lemon: Resilience Through Sour Seasons 141

Chapter 12: The Pear: Balance And Wholeness 156

Conclusion: The Harvest – Raising A Fruitful Generation 172

FRUIT OF THE WOMB

INTRODUCTION

"Lo, children are an heritage of the Lord: and the fruit of the womb is his reward." (Psalm 127:3)

Every orchard begins with a seed, small, fragile, and easily overlooked, yet filled with generations of sweetness and shade. Within its shell lies potential unseen by the untrained eye: the promise of harvests that can nourish multitudes. So, it is with children.

When God entrusts a child into the arms of a parent, He plants not only a life but a legacy. Every child is a divine seed, fearfully and wonderfully made, uniquely designed, full of purpose that must be nurtured, guided, and protected. Parenting is not an accident of biology; it is the sacred calling of cultivation. Like a farmer tending his field, every parent must learn the rhythms of soil and season, sowing, watering, waiting, and harvesting in faith.

Yet parenting is rarely neat or predictable. Children, like fruit, come in varieties. Some are tender like *strawberries,* others resilient like *lemons.* Some grow in clusters like *bananas,* others in layers of mystery like *coconuts.* Each carries sweetness to delight, sourness to challenge, seeds of legacy hidden within, and fragile skins that bruise if handled carelessly. To raise children well is to enter God's orchard and learn the wisdom of cultivation.

In our modern age, parenting often becomes reactive instead of intentional. Many hope their children will "turn out right" without deliberate effort, while others pour their energy into one area: academics, athletics, or behavior, neglecting other vital dimensions of growth. The result is children who grow unevenly: brilliant in one area but broken in another. Yet Scripture paints a different picture. *"Jesus grew in wisdom and stature, and in favor with God and man."* (Luke 2:52) In one verse, we glimpse the fullness of God's design intellectual growth, physical health, spiritual depth, and relational maturity. Balanced, whole, and fruitful. This is the pattern of divine parenting: the way of the orchard.

To parent with purpose is to see children the way God sees them, not as problems to be fixed or trophies to be displayed, but as seeds to be cultivated into harvests of faith, character, and fruitfulness.

Why fruit? Because fruit is the language God often uses to describe human flourishing. Jesus said, *"By their fruit you will recognize them."* (Matthew 7:16) Paul wrote that *"the fruit of the Spirit is love, joy, peace, patience, kindness, goodness, faithfulness, gentleness, and self-control."* (Galatians 5:22-23) Psalm 1 describes the righteous as a tree planted by streams of water, *"which yields its fruit in season."* Even the Great Commission echoes this principle of fruitfulness: disciples who make disciples, lives reproducing righteousness across generations.

Fruit, then, is not merely food. It is *symbol, sustenance, and story.* And when we look closely at the fruits God placed in creation, we discover living parables about the growth of children.

The *apple* teaches us about innocence and sweetness. The *banana* reminds us that growth happens in community. The *grape* speaks of connection and fruitfulness through abiding in Christ. The *pineapple* combines strength and hospitality, teaching that resilience and kindness can coexist. The *orange* reveals wholeness, segments distinct yet united, the *strawberry* whispers of tenderness and humility, thriving close to the ground. The *coconut* teaches patience and the beauty of discovering hidden layers. The *lemon* challenges us with sour seasons that build resilience. The *pear* embodies balance and harmony.

Each fruit preaches a sermon, each reveals a principle, each carries a lesson for the heart of a parent.

Parenting, therefore, is not about raising children for the applause of men but for the pleasure of God. Diplomas may decorate walls, and trophies may fill shelves, but these are not the ultimate fruit. What of the heart that is unloved, undisciplined, or unanchored in Christ?

FRUIT OF THE WOMB

Proper parenting is not measured by worldly success but by eternal legacy, fruit that remains.

Deuteronomy 6 calls parents to impress God's Word on their children, to speak of it when sitting at home, walking along the road, lying down, and rising. This is not casual parenting. It is deliberate cultivation, sowing truth daily until it takes root and bears fruit. It embraces both the sweetness and the sourness, the joy of harvest and the labor of sowing. It recognizes that even the difficult seasons are divine tools for shaping resilience, compassion, and godliness.

This book is not a technical manual, nor a sentimental collection of memories. It is a *biblical meditation* woven with *practical wisdom,* an orchard of lessons for those entrusted with the heritage of children. Here you will find encouragement when the work feels weary, perspective when the seasons grow sour, and renewed vision when the harvest seems far away. You will be reminded that every tantrum, every laugh, every question, and every tear has purpose. Nothing is wasted in God's garden.

Picture the harvest table: apples, oranges, grapes, pears, pineapples, strawberries, coconuts, and lemons, each unique, each needed, each carrying seed for more. Now picture your children: different personalities, different strengths, different stages, yet each placed in your hands as a gift from God. The goal of parenting is not to make them identical or perfect, but to cultivate them into fruitful lives, each bearing their God-given sweetness, resilience, and balance.

And when the harvest comes, when they stand as adults of faith, integrity, and love, you will taste the joy of knowing your labor was not in vain.

Welcome to the orchard.

To raise a child is to tend the garden of God — a sacred act of faith that turns today's seeds into tomorrow's legacy.

CHAPTER 1

THE APPLE — SWEETNESS AND INNOCENCE

Every fruit God created speaks a language of life and purpose. The apple, crisp, fragrant, and familiar, embodies the earliest and tender stage of human growth: childhood. Its sweetness mirrors innocence; its delicate skin suggests vulnerability; its hidden seeds symbolize potential.

Children, like apples, refresh the world. Their laughter renews weary hearts; their trust softens hardened spirits. In their purity, we glimpse *Eden*, an echo of what humanity once was and what God still calls us to become.

The Language of Innocence

The psalmist prayed, *"Keep me as the apple of Your eye; hide me under the shadow of Your wings"* (Psalm 17:8, KJV). The "apple of the eye" refers to the pupil, the most guarded part of our vision. It represents what is most cherished and most vulnerable. In that image, God reveals how He values His children: loved, watched, and protected.

Children enter the world carrying this divine signature of purity. They are open, curious, unpretentious, and profoundly trusting. Jesus affirmed their sacredness: *"Truly I tell you, unless you change and become like little children, you will never enter the kingdom of heaven"* (Matthew 18:3, NIV). The humility and openness that mark a child are the very attitudes that open heaven's doors.

But innocence is fragile. Modern life rushes what should unfold gently. Screens expose, lyrics desensitize, and peer culture glamorizes rebellion. Exposure masquerades as maturity; precociousness is mistaken for wisdom. Scripture calls parents not to panic but to discern: *"Above all else, guard your heart, for everything you do flows from it"* (Proverbs 4:23, NIV). To guard a heart is not to hide it away but to train it, to help a child distinguish truth from counterfeit, sweetness from decay.

Parenting, at its essence, is the stewardship of innocence. God modeled this stewardship in *Eden*: *"The LORD God took the man and put him in the Garden of Eden to work it and take care of it"* (Genesis 2:15, NIV). "Work" means to nurture; "keep" means to guard. Every home becomes a miniature *Eden* where parents cultivate and protect young hearts.

FRUIT OF THE WOMB

In practice, this stewardship looks like predictable routines, affection wrapped in boundaries, and conversations that center truth. When parents read bedtime stories, pray at the table, or pause to explain right from wrong, they are tending the garden of innocence. These daily moments are sacred maintenance.

Developmentally, innocence corresponds to the first stage of emotional growth, *trust*. Psychologists such as Erik Erikson describe it as the foundation upon which every later capacity—empathy, confidence, faith—rests. Infants learn whether the world is safe through the rhythm of response. When caregivers are steady and affectionate, children form secure attachments; they interpret life through stability and kindness. When care is inconsistent or harsh, fear becomes the soil of experience, and innocence withers.

God's own parenting models this. *"As a father has compassion on his children, so the LORD has compassion on those who fear Him"* (Psalm 103:13, NIV). Compassion is consistency wrapped in gentleness. Parents imitate divine compassion when they create atmospheres of predictable love. Correction, when necessary, is delivered without humiliation. Encouragement, when offered, strengthens rather than flatters.

A child learns God's nature from a parent's tone before they ever memorize Scripture. A calm, *no* unspoken word of love communicates that limits can coexist with safety. In those early years, parental presence becomes theology with skin on it.

Innocence, however, is not naivety. It is moral clarity unpolluted by cynicism. Children are born with an innate sense of wonder; they marvel at ants marching, clouds shifting, or prayer whispered before sleep. Adults lose this wonder through overexposure, yet Jesus points back to it as the gateway to faith. To cultivate innocence is to preserve that capacity to marvel at God's world while gradually teaching discernment.

When we rush children past wonder, we rob them of worship. Curiosity is the doorway to praise. Every *time* a child asks about God's world is an early sermon on divine design. To dismiss it with irritation is to silence a budding theologian. Patience transforms questions into spiritual mentoring moments.

The sweetness of childhood also invites parents to rediscover their own softness. Each giggle, drawing, and bedtime confession becomes an altar of gratitude. In those moments, parents glimpse themselves as God's children, equally dependent and equally cherished. To become like little children is not regression but restoration of childlike trust in the father's love.

When parents protect innocence, they mirror heaven's rhythm: steadiness, kindness, and truth. An apple cannot grow in polluted soil, and neither can innocence thrive in chaos. Homes saturated with peace, laughter, and forgiveness become orchards of grace.

The Anatomy of Character

Every apple has three parts: skin, flesh, and core. Character mirrors this design through boundaries, substance, and convictions. Parents are not sculptors forcing form; they are gardeners drawing out what God already designed. *"You made all the delicate, inner parts of my body and knit me together in my mother's womb"* (Psalm 139:13, NLT). Children are divine architecture in progress.

Boundaries as Skin

The skin protects sweetness. Without it, fruit bruises; without structure, children collapse under the weight of freedom. When parents set clear expectations about words, respect, digital habits, and time, they communicate worth: *"You are valuable enough to guide."* Discipline, when loving, becomes dignity in motion.

"Whoever spares the rod hates their children, but the one who loves their children is careful to discipline them" (Proverbs 13:24, NIV). The "rod" here is not a weapon but a measure, a shepherd's staff that nudges, not injures. Proper discipline protects destiny; it does not punish curiosity.

FRUIT OF THE WOMB

Modern parenting often swings between permissiveness and harsh control. Neither nurtures wholeness. Grace-filled firmness is the balance of heaven. Children flourish where authority and affection hold hands. When correction is calm and boundaries consistent, a child's nervous system learns safety in structure. That calm predictability literally shapes the developing brain toward resilience and empathy.

Substance as Flesh

Beneath the skin is nourishment. The flesh of character is what children digest from everyday life: truth, patience, affection, and example. Children rarely remember our lectures, but they always remember how they felt in our presence. If we want grateful, secure, and kind adults, we must become living examples of those fruits. *"The righteous lead blameless lives; blessed are their children after them"* (Proverbs 20:7, NIV). Integrity feeds the soul; hypocrisy starves it.

When parents practice honesty in small things, apologizing for impatience, keeping promises, and giving thanks, they teach moral nutrition. Faith is caught before it is taught. We cannot expect children to crave what they have never seen us enjoy.

Discipline shapes appetite. Children raised with grace learn that limits are love and obedience leads to peace. *"No discipline seems pleasant at the time, but painful. Later on, however, it produces a harvest of righteousness and peace for those who have been trained by it"* (Hebrews 12:11, NIV). Notice the word *trained,* discipline is developmental, not destructive. It trains the taste buds of the soul to find sweetness in what is right.

Convictions as Core

The apple's core holds seeds, future orchards in miniature. Convictions are those seeds. They determine what will grow long after parents are gone. *"Train up a child in the way he should go [teaching him to seek God's wisdom and will for his abilities and talents]; even when he is old, he will not depart from it"* (Proverbs 22:6, AMP). Training is planting; consistency is watering; prayer is sunlight.

Moral psychologists call this stage *internalization*—when outer rules become an inner compass. Between ages six and ten, a child begins saying, "I tell the truth because I am honest." That shift is sacred. Parents who confess their own failures teach integrity as authenticity, not performance. Rules without relationship breed rebellion; guidance wrapped in love breeds maturity.

When parents fail, and every parent does, the way they repair the relationship becomes the most powerful lesson of all. A heartfelt apology, a hug after misunderstanding, a moment of laughter after tears, these are seeds of emotional resilience. Character is not built by perfection but by repair.

Faith anchors the core. *"I am the Vine; you are the branches. When you're joined with Me and I with you, the relation intimate and organic, the harvest is sure to be abundant"* (John 15:5, The Message). Connection to Christ roots conscience beyond culture. Parents strengthen that connection by weaving faith into ordinary rhythms such as reading Scripture over breakfast, praying before bedtime, blessing children before school, and singing together in the car. These small rituals build spiritual muscle memory. They tell the child, *"Faith is not a Sunday performance; it's the air we breathe."*

Character is tested in conflict. Children who experience gentle correction and empathetic listening develop resilience. They learn that mistakes are not moral collapse but invitations to learn. When parents model apology and forgiveness, they teach the language of restoration. When they manage anger with patience, they teach self-control. These micro-moments, naming feelings, calming before reacting, choosing reconciliation, form the emotional architecture of identity.

Paul described this moral anatomy: *"The fruit of the Spirit is love, joy, peace, forbearance, kindness, goodness, faithfulness, gentleness and self-control"* (Galatians 5:22-23, NIV). These virtues are the nutrients of lasting character, sweetness that endures when outer charm fades. A child rooted in love and truth can withstand pressure without losing purity. Like a well-kept apple, their faith stays crisp even under weight.

The Orchard and Its Legacy

Every apple points back to its tree, and every tree to its orchard. Children bear the imprint of the homes and communities that nurture them. *"Children are a heritage from the LORD, offspring a reward from Him"* (Psalm 127:3, NIV). Heritage means inheritance, what God entrusts to multiply. Parenting is not ownership; it is a partnership with the Creator.

Legacy is seasonal. *"That person is like a tree planted by streams of water, which yields its fruit in season and whose leaf does not wither"* (Psalm 1:3, NIV). Fruit develops in its time. Some seasons bring visible obedience; others require silent faith. The promise stands: *"Let us not become weary in doing good, for at the proper time we will reap a harvest if we do not give up"* (Galatians 6:9, NIV). Endurance is love wearing work clothes.

The orchard also speaks of community. No tree thrives alone. Families need fellowship, grandparents, mentors, teachers, and friends who reinforce godly values. *"Iron sharpens iron; so a man sharpens the countenance of his friend"* (Proverbs 27:17, KJV). Parents sharpen one another through prayer circles, shared meals, and honest conversation. Isolation breeds burnout; community replenishes joy.

Scripture paints generational faith as a living chain: *"When I call to remembrance the genuine faith that is in you, which dwelt first in thy grandmother Lois and thy mother Eunice; and I am persuaded that in thee also"* (2 Timothy 1:5, KJV). Timothy's faith was cultivated by example, not by accident. Every act of consistency, a parent's prayer, a grandmother's story, a teacher's encouragement, plants shade for tomorrow's children.

Our culture urges parents to measure success by speed and status, but God measures it by fruit. True legacy is not what we hand to our children but what we sow within them. When we model humility, gratitude, and generosity, we plant virtues that outlive income. Children who watch parents serve rather than strive, forgive rather than retaliate, and give rather than grasp learn the secret of heaven's economy: increase comes through surrender.

Protecting the Orchard

Every orchard faces pests: comparison, cynicism, consumerism. Parents guard their spiritual trees by cultivating gratitude. Gratitude turns scarcity into sufficiency and redirects a family's gaze from what they lack to *Who provides*. When parents confess envy and replace it with thanksgiving, they prune the weeds of discontent. A thankful home produces content hearts.

Guarding legacy also means guarding time. The pace of modern life erodes presence. Families often live in the same house but on different screens. To preserve connection, parents must model Sabbath, unhurried moments when laughter replaces notifications. The Sabbath table, like an orchard bench, is where sweetness is shared.

Ultimately, legacy requires release. *"Like arrows in the hands of a warrior are children born in one's youth"* (Psalm 127:4, NIV). Arrows are made to fly. Parents who have prayed, taught, and modeled truth can let go with peace. The apple must fall but not far from righteousness. We release children not to independence from God but into intimacy with Him.

In God's design, every generation becomes seed for the next. Families who live by faith transform neighborhoods. Churches that nurture families heal nations. When parents raise children who walk in sweetness and integrity, they extend the orchard of God's kingdom across the earth. The apple is not merely fruit; it is testimony. Sweetness preserved becomes strength transmitted. Character cultivated becomes legacy extended. What God plants in one generation, He intends to multiply in the next.

FRUIT OF THE WOMB

Reflection Questions

1. In what ways does my child or the children I influence reflect the sweetness and innocence of an apple?

2. What practical steps can I take to guard my child's heart and protect their innocence in today's culture?

3. How am I shaping the *core* of my child's character through discipline, encouragement, and example?

4. Do I see my children only for the present joy they bring or also as carriers of seeds for future generations?

5. How can I make God's Word taste *sweet* and desirable to my child each day?

A Prayer of Blessing

Heavenly Father, thank You for the gift of children, the apples of our eyes and the heritage of Your kingdom. Help me cherish their sweetness, protect their innocence, and nourish their hearts with Your Word. Strengthen me as a parent to shape their character, preserve their joy, and guide their steps toward You. May the seeds of potential within them grow into orchards of righteousness that bless generations to come. I declare that my children are fruitful, protected, and rooted in Your love. In Jesus' name, Amen.

FRUIT OF THE WOMB

Practical Family Activity – Apple Night

1. Buy a variety of apples, red, green, and yellow. Wash and slice them for tasting.

2. As a family, taste each apple and discuss how each one has different flavors but all are sweet and nourishing.

3. Connect this to the lesson: *God made every child unique, but each one is valuable and refreshing.*

4. Parents pray over each child, declaring them the *apple of God's eye* and speaking blessings over their lives.

5. End by planting an apple seed in a small pot as a symbol of growth and future potential.

CHAPTER 2

THE MANGO: RICHNESS OF DESTINY

Among all fruits, the mango stands apart, radiant, fragrant, and filled with golden richness. Known across cultures as the *king of fruits*, it represents abundance, maturity, and the joy that comes through process. In the same way, every child carries a richness within, placed there by the hand of God. Children are not born as empty vessels to be filled; they are divine masterpieces, already carrying the seed of destiny.

The psalmist captures this wonder in *Psalm 139:13-14* (NIV), saying, *"For You created my inmost being; You knit me together in my mother's womb. I praise You because I am fearfully and wonderfully made; Your works are wonderful; I know that full well."* These words remind us that a child's design is intentional. Just as every mango has a distinct texture and flavor, no two children are alike. God did not mass-produce humanity; He crafted each soul with purpose.

A mango's sweetness does not appear overnight. It begins green and firm, exposed to rain, sun, and changing seasons. With time, its color deepens, and its fragrance matures. Likewise, a child's potential unfolds gradually. Early stages may seem ordinary or even awkward, yet beneath the surface, God's hand is shaping something extraordinary. Parents must resist the temptation to rush the ripening process. The same patience that matures a mango's flesh also matures a child's faith, character, and gifts.

Inside every mango lies a large, immovable seed. You cannot enjoy the fruit without meeting the core, a reminder that destiny lies at the center of every child's being. God said to Jeremiah, *"Before I formed you in the womb I knew you, before you were born, I set you apart; I appointed you as a prophet to the nations"* (Jeremiah 1:5, NIV). This verse unveils the truth that destiny precedes birth. Before a child ever takes a breath, heaven has already whispered purpose over their life.

Parents are not the inventors of destiny; they are its stewards. Just as a gardener does not decide what kind of tree a seed will become, a parent cannot dictate what their child must be; they can only cultivate what God already placed inside. The mango tree is determined by its seed. Likewise, a child's spiritual DNA — their temperament, passion, and giftings, is pre-written by their Creator.

Even in psychology, this aligns with what researchers call intrinsic motivation, the internal drive that points a child toward their natural strengths. A young boy who loves to build may carry the seed of design or engineering. A girl who consoles others easily may bear a pastoral or healing gift. These instincts are not random; they are whispers of divine destiny.

Proverbs 22:6 (AMP) encourages, *"Train up a child in the way he should go [teaching him to seek God's wisdom and will for his abilities and talents], even when he is old, he will not depart from it."* This scripture implies individual pathways, the way he should go, not the way others went. Each child's variety must be discerned and nurtured accordingly. Just as the Kent mango thrives in tropical heat and the Julie mango prefers coastal air, each child's development blossoms under the right spiritual and emotional climate.

The early years of childhood are like the mango's blossom season, delicate, fragrant, and vulnerable. Blossoms must be shielded from strong winds and insects. In the same way, a child's innocence requires protection. Jesus Himself valued this purity when He said, *"Let the little children come to Me, and do not hinder them, for the kingdom of heaven belongs to such as these"* (Matthew 19:14, NIV).

That statement reveals both divine affection and parental assignment. The innocence of children is not weakness; it is heaven's reflection, the mirror of God's intent before sin entered the world. When parents guard innocence, they are safeguarding the original image of God.

FRUIT OF THE WOMB

This is why childhood faith is so powerful. Children believe before they analyze, trust before they fear, and love before they calculate. Their capacity for faith is their greatest treasure. Parents must therefore build spiritual environments that strengthen this trust through prayer, song, story, and presence. Faith that is nurtured early becomes conviction that endures later.

When God places a seed within a child, He expects guardians to tend it carefully. *Genesis 2:15* (NIV) says, *"The Lord God took the man and put him in the Garden of Eden to work it and take care of it."* That same dual instruction, to work and to keep, applies to parenting. To *work* is to nurture: provide, teach, and encourage. To *keep* is to guard: protect from influences that corrupt the soul. Every home, then, becomes a garden where the seeds of destiny are both cultivated and defended.

A mango farmer knows not every blossom becomes fruit, and not every fruit matures perfectly. The same is true for parenting. Yet the faithful gardener remains consistent, watering daily, pruning gently, and waiting for the harvest. For in every child entrusted to us, there is a seed heaven refuses to waste.

FRUIT OF THE WOMB

Cultivating Richness *Parenting as the Gardener's Work*

If the mango represents destiny, the parent represents the gardener. A mango tree left untended grows unevenly. It may produce fruit, but of poor quality. Likewise, children require consistent care, structure, correction, affirmation, and prayer to bring forth the richness within.

Proverbs 13:24 (NIV) teaches, *"Whoever spares the rod hates their children, but the one who loves their children is careful to discipline them."* The word *rod* here does not imply harsh punishment but careful guidance. The loving parent disciplines not to harm but to direct, trimming attitudes and behaviors that hinder growth, much like pruning a branch that blocks sunlight.

At the same time, mango trees thrive in warmth, not just correction. Too much pruning without sunshine weakens the tree. Similarly, too much criticism without affection discourages a child. *Proverbs 16:24* (KJV) reminds us, *"Pleasant words are as a honeycomb, sweet to the soul, and health to the bones."* Encouragement and kindness are as vital as discipline.

Every *time I'm proud of you, I see God's hand on your life*, or *You did well* becomes sunlight that ripens the fruit of confidence. Psychological research supports this biblical wisdom: children thrive where love is expressed verbally and physically. Insecure children often come from homes where silence replaced affirmation. Words, like light, awaken growth.

Parenting is both science and spirit, both labor and love. It demands patience, observation, and divine partnership. A farmer cannot make a mango grow by shouting at it. He must nurture the conditions. Likewise, a parent cannot rush character. They must create the right environment for it to emerge.

When frustration tempts us to give up, *Galatians 6:9* (NIV) encourages, *"Let us not become weary in doing good, for at the proper time we will reap a harvest if we do not give up."* Parenting is a long obedience in the same direction, a daily watering of words, example, and prayer.

Children learn far more by observation than by instruction. When they watch parents pray before reacting, forgive when hurt, or persevere when tired, they internalize those virtues. The home becomes a living classroom where destiny takes shape through example.

Ecclesiastes 3:1 (NIV) reminds us, *"There is a time for everything, and a season for every activity under the heavens."* Parenting, too, has seasons: the years of protection, the years of preparation, and the years of release. The wise parent discerns each season and adjusts their hands accordingly: firm when pruning, open when releasing.

FRUIT OF THE WOMB

A mango farmer knows when to stop watering and start waiting. Parents must do the same, knowing when to step back so their child can practice what was taught. It is in those moments of trust that faith matures and destiny begins to show color.

Harvest of Purpose *When Destiny Comes to Fruition*

When a mango tree finally ripens its fruit, the air itself seems to change. The fragrance draws people near long before anyone sees the fruit hanging from its branches. Destiny works the same way. When it begins to mature, its aroma influences others. You do not have to announce it. Others will sense it.

Ephesians 2:10 (NIV) declares, *"For we are God's handiwork, created in Christ Jesus to do good works, which God prepared in advance for us to do."* Just as every mango tree is planted for a future harvest, every child is created for divine assignments prepared long before they are aware of them. When that purpose ripens, the sweetness of their life refreshes everyone around them.

A ripe mango does not struggle to prove its value. Its flavor speaks for itself. Likewise, a mature child of God does not chase validation. Their character and fruit testify to divine workmanship. Jesus said, *"You did not choose Me, but I chose you and appointed you so that you might go and bear fruit, fruit that will last"* (John 15:16, NIV). Fruit that lasts is influence that continues after seasons change, decisions, attitudes, and legacies that remain fragrant long after our words fade.

Parents must remember that fruit is never for the tree itself. A mango tree does not eat its own mangoes. Its fruit blesses others. So too, a child's destiny is not merely for personal gain but for service to others. When a child learns early that their talents are gifts meant to bless the world, they begin to see success through the lens of stewardship rather than status.

Jesus captured this truth in *Luke 6:38* (NLT): *"Give, and you will receive. Your gift will return to you in full, pressed down, shaken together to make room for more, running over, and poured into your lap. The amount you give will determine the amount you get back."* Children who learn generosity grow into adults whose lives multiply richness wherever they go.

The mango's journey from blossom to fruit reminds us that every stage matters. Early faith, small obedience's, and quiet acts of kindness are all part of the process. Parents can celebrate unseen progress as much as visible achievement, the moment a child apologizes sincerely, chooses truth over convenience, or comforts a friend. These are the ripening signs of destiny in action.

God rejoices in such growth. *Zechariah 4:10* (NLT) says, *"Do not despise these small beginnings, for the Lord rejoices to see the work begin."* Each tiny step of maturity is evidence that the seed of destiny is alive and growing.

When children begin to bear fruit, parents must learn the art of release. Hannah modeled this beautifully when she brought young Samuel back to the temple, saying, *"I prayed for this child, and the Lord has granted me what I asked of Him. So now I give him to the Lord. For his whole life he will be given over to the Lord"* (1 Samuel 1:27-28, NIV). Her surrender did not mean abandonment but confidence that God would finish what He started.

Every parent faces their own Hannah moment, releasing a child to college, marriage, ministry, or purpose beyond home. It is both joy and ache, pride and prayer. Yet the mango must fall from the branch to reproduce. If it clings too long, it rots. Likewise, overprotection can suffocate growth. Trust releases maturity.

Psalm 1:3 (NIV) paints a fitting picture, *"That person is like a tree planted by streams of water, which yields its fruit in season and whose leaf does not wither. Whatever they do prospers."* Parents who have nurtured faithfully can rest in that promise. If the roots were watered with Scripture and love, the fruit will appear in season.

When Destiny Blesses Others

The actual test of maturity is not success but service. Joseph's destiny did not reach fulfillment when he received his colorful coat.

FRUIT OF THE WOMB

It matured when he saved nations. Esther's calling was not crowned the day she became queen but the day she risked her life to deliver her people. Their sweetness fed others.

Destiny always moves outward. It nourishes families, churches, workplaces, and nations. *Proverbs 11:25* (NLT) reminds us, *"The generous will prosper; those who refresh others will themselves be refreshed."* Every parent's prayer should be that their children grow into such people, lives that refresh others.

To cultivate that spirit, families can model generosity together: serving meals to neighbors, giving time at church, or simply sharing stories of God's goodness. These moments teach that our blessings are meant to flow. The same tree that bears fruit this year drops seeds for next season's harvest.

The mango also teaches endurance. Fruit trees face storms, pests, and seasons of drought, yet they remain standing. In the same way, destiny matures through difficulty. *Romans 5:3–4* (NIV) reminds us, *"We also glory in our sufferings, because we know that suffering produces perseverance; perseverance, character; and character, hope."* When children face disappointment, parents can help them interpret hardship not as punishment but as pruning. God never wastes pain. He turns it into strength.

As fruit matures, its color deepens. So too, as a child's destiny ripens, their character takes on new hues of humility, wisdom, and compassion. They begin to resemble their Maker. *Colossians 1:10* (NLT) says, *"Then the way you live will always honor and please the Lord, and your lives will produce every kind of good fruit. All the while, you will grow as you learn to know God better and better."*

This is the ultimate goal of parenting, not to raise successful children, but fruitful ones, lives that honor God and bless others.

Reflection Questions

1. How can I identify and affirm the unique *flavor* of richness in my child rather than comparing them to others?

2. In what ways am I helping to cultivate the *seed of destiny* at my child's core through love, discipline, and prayer?

3. Are there areas where I might be neglecting or over-controlling my child's path instead of discerning God's design?

4. How am I sowing generosity and godly character that will impact future generations?

5. What sacrifices might God be asking me to make today so that my child's destiny can flourish tomorrow?

FRUIT OF THE WOMB

A Prayer of Blessing

Father, thank You for the richness You have placed in every child You entrust to us. Like the mango, they are full of sweetness and carry a great *seed of destiny* within them. Help me to see their uniqueness through Your eyes, to affirm their gifts, to prune with gentleness, and to cultivate their character with patience and prayer. Protect them from every influence that would choke their calling and let their destiny ripen in Your perfect timing. May their lives nourish others, bless generations, and bring glory to Your name.

In Jesus' name, Amen.

Practical Family Activity — *Mango Destiny Night*

1. Share fresh mango slices as a family. Before eating, hold up the mango seed and talk about how large and central it is.

2. Explain to children, *"Just as this mango has a big seed, God has placed a great destiny inside of you."*

3. Each family member speaks one positive trait they see in the child, such as kindness, creativity, or leadership.

4. Parents pray aloud over each child's destiny, laying hands on them as a sign of blessing and dedication.

5. End by writing a short *Destiny Journal Entry* for each child, recording the words of affirmation and prayer shared that

night. Keep these journal pages as a family treasure to revisit during future milestones.

CHAPTER 3

THE BANANA: GROWTH IN CLUSTERS

Among all the fruits God created, few illustrate community more beautifully than the banana. Bananas never grow alone; they appear in bunches suspended from one central stalk, each fruit curving upward toward the light. Their growth pattern embodies the very rhythm of creation—life joined to life, strength drawn from togetherness.

From the moment of birth, every human being mirrors this divine pattern. An infant's first instinct is to reach for connection, to feel the warmth of a mother's touch, the steadiness of a father's voice, the reassurance of presence. Before a child learns to speak, they already understand what it means to belong. This design for a relationship is not accidental; it is sacred. Genesis 2:18 (NIV) declares, "The LORD God said, 'It is not good for the man to be alone.'" God's first human pronouncement against loneliness predates sin; it reveals that isolation contradicts His nature.

Children, then, are born for community. They flourish when surrounded by love, structure, and faith, but they wither when left emotionally unattended. Like bananas pulled prematurely from their bunch, children separated from nurturing relationships ripen too quickly and spoil before their time. Their emotional and spiritual balance depends on being rooted among others who reflect God's heart.

Ecclesiastes 4:9 10 (NLT) reminds us, "Two people are better off than one, for they can help each other succeed. If one person falls, the other can reach out and help. But someone who falls alone is in real trouble." The wisdom writer speaks of companionship as protection. When a child falls, whether in discouragement, temptation, or failure, someone present to lift them can make the difference between recovery and ruin.

Belonging does more than comfort; it defines identity. Psalm 68:6 (NIV) proclaims, "God sets the lonely in families." He places children in relational clusters to teach them who they are and whose they are. A banana draws shape from the curve of those beside it; so, too, children form character from those nearest to them.

In a generation increasingly shaped by technology, the danger of artificial connection looms large. Screens glow while hearts remain untouched. Yet Scripture insists that faith and family require shared space, shared meals, shared words. Deuteronomy 6:6-7 (NIV) says, "These commandments that I give you today are to be on your hearts. Impress them on your children. Talk about them when you sit at home and when you walk along the road, when you lie down and when you get up." Truth is transmitted not through lectures but through life together, conversations that flow naturally within the cluster of daily fellowship.

Psychologists confirm what Scripture long taught: secure attachment fosters confidence, empathy, and faith. When children experience consistent love and dependable care, they interpret the world as safe and trustworthy. That security becomes the foundation of moral development and spiritual openness. Psalm 103:13 (NIV) echoes this divine pattern: "As a father has compassion on his children, so the LORD has compassion on those who fear Him."

Parents who model compassionate steadiness teach children what God's love feels like. Their presence builds invisible scaffolding inside the soul, a structure strong enough to withstand the pressures of adolescence and adulthood. To belong is to be seen and valued; to parent is to become the mirror of belonging.

Bananas bend upward as they grow, following the pull of sunlight. Children do the same. They rise toward what they see consistently. When homes are filled with peace, when churches live in unity, when communities honor righteousness, children naturally incline toward light. The family bunch becomes a living parable of grace curving heavenward.

The Power and Fragility of Togetherness

FRUIT OF THE WOMB

Togetherness is a sacred strength, yet it must be handled gently. The same bunch that protects each banana can also bruise it if compressed too tightly. Likewise, the family or community that surrounds a child must balance structure with sensitivity, boundaries with tenderness.

A banana's soft skin reminds us that children are impressionable. Harshness leaves marks not easily erased. Colossians 3:21 (AMP) warns, "Fathers, do not provoke or irritate or exasperate your children [with demands that are trivial or unreasonable or humiliating or abusive]; do not be hard on them or harass them, so that they will not lose heart and become discouraged or unmotivated [with their spirit broken]."

Gentle correction, not constant criticism, cultivates maturity. Proverbs 15:1 (NLT) says, "A gentle answer deflects anger, but harsh words make tempers flare." Parents who discipline through calm explanation and consistent love build trust instead of fear. Discipline detached from love hardens the heart; discipline rooted in relationship shapes it.

The banana bunch also shields each fruit from direct sun and heavy rain. Its layered structure distributes pressure evenly. Families and faith communities function the same way: they absorb the shocks of life together. When one member suffers, others intercede; when one falters, others steady. Proverbs 11:14 (NIV) affirms, "Where there is no guidance, a nation falls, but victory is won through many advisers." Safety multiplies in counsel.

Children growing within godly clusters learn that protection is not control, it is covering. Covering provides room to stretch while staying safe. In the wilderness, Israel survived because tribes camped around the presence of God; each family had a position, but all shared the same center. Likewise, Christian families thrive when Christ remains the center around whom all relationships orbit.

Isolation, however, distorts growth. A banana detached from its bunch ripens faster but decays sooner. Similarly, children who are emotionally or spiritually detached may appear independent but often carry unhealed emptiness. Proverbs 18:1 (NKJV) cautions, "A man who isolates himself seeks his own desire; he rages against all wise judgment." Independence without accountability breeds fragility disguised as strength.

Gentleness, therefore, is not weakness but wisdom. Ephesians 6:4 (AMP) instructs, "Fathers, do not provoke your children to anger [to the point of resentment with demands that are trivial or unreasonable], but bring them up [tenderly, with lovingkindness] in the discipline and instruction of the Lord." Parental firmness rooted in kindness preserves innocence and encourages obedience born of love, not fear.

Bananas ripen at different paces within the same bunch. One may turn golden while another remains green. Such diversity within unity reflects divine wisdom. Philippians 1:6 (NIV) assures, "He who began a good work in you will carry it on to completion until the day of Christ Jesus." Parents must allow God's timing to unfold uniquely in each child. Comparison poisons growth; patience perfects it.

Communal living also refines humility. Children in clusters learn cooperation, forgiveness, and empathy, the social fruit of the Spirit. Galatians 5:22–23 (NIV) lists these as evidence of maturity: "Love, joy, peace, forbearance, kindness, goodness, faithfulness, gentleness and self-control." These virtues do not develop in solitude; they ripen through daily interaction.

The church community contributes another protective layer. Hebrews 10:24 25 (MSG) urges believers to stay engaged: "Let's see how inventive we can be in encouraging love and helping out, not avoiding worshiping together as some do but spurring each other on." When children grow accustomed to worshiping, learning, and serving with others, their spiritual roots deepen beyond family walls.

Togetherness, then, is both a shield and a shaping tool. It preserves sweetness and promotes strength. Children nurtured within prayerful clusters seldom fall alone; someone's faith catches them. Like bananas supported by their bunch, they mature evenly, gracefully, and with a steady color of character.

Growing Strong in the Cluster — Generational and Spiritual Continuity

Every banana bunch draws life from one root system. Although multiple hands of fruit hang separately, they share one stem. This unseen connection symbolizes how families, churches, and generations draw sustenance from a shared spiritual root, God Himself. *John 15:5* (MSG) captures it clearly: *"I am the Vine, you are the branches. When you're joined with me and I with you, the relation intimate and organic, the harvest is sure to be abundant."*

Children thrive when their cluster remains rooted in Christ. They may belong to family, school, and community, but only in Christ do those relationships find eternal cohesion. Without Him, the cluster becomes a social structure without spiritual sap; with Him, it becomes a living fellowship nourished by grace.

This is why spiritual formation begins early. *Deuteronomy 6 6 - 7* commands parents to impress God's words on their children: *"Talk about them when you sit at home and when you walk along the road, when you lie down and when you get up."* Faith is not a Sunday ritual; it is a family rhythm. When Scripture saturates daily conversation, children come to see God not as a distant deity but as a near companion.

A cluster rooted in worship becomes a sanctuary. In such homes, prayer is as natural as breathing. Worship is not confined to church walls but rises from breakfast tables, bedtime prayers, and spontaneous songs. These environments cultivate resilience. *Psalm 133:1* (NIV) declares, *"How good and pleasant it is when God's people live together in unity!"* Unity produces oil, anointing that flows freely where peace reigns. Children raised under that oil of unity carry spiritual fragrance into every space they enter.

The banana plant also multiplies through new shoots that sprout from its base, called *suckers*. These offshoots ensure continual fruitfulness even after one stalk has completed its season. This is a picture of generational continuity. When parents live faithfully before their children, they reproduce righteousness naturally. *Psalm 145:4* (NLT) says, *"Let each generation tell its children of your mighty acts; let them proclaim your power."*

Children absorb values more by observation than instruction. When they watch their parents pray through difficulty, forgive offenses, or serve faithfully, they internalize truth beyond words. They learn that belonging to a cluster means carrying both privilege and responsibility. They see that spiritual inheritance is not genetic; it is cultivated through example.

Families that stay united in Christ become living testimonies of divine faithfulness. Even when individual members falter, the cluster's collective faith restores them. *Galatians 6:1–2* (NIV) teaches, *"Brothers and sisters, if someone is caught in a sin, you who live by the Spirit should restore that person gently… Carry each other's burdens, and in this way you will fulfill the law of Christ."* Restoration happens in clusters, not in isolation.

God's design for community extends beyond bloodlines into the wider household of faith. The Church becomes an extended bunch where spiritual fathers, mothers, and peers nurture one another. *Ephesians 4:16* (AMP) beautifully captures this: *"From Him the whole body [the church, in all its various parts], joined and knitted firmly together by what every joint supplies, when each part is working properly, causes the body to grow and mature."*

Children who grow within such clusters become emotionally balanced, spiritually stable, and socially mature. They learn to submit without losing individuality, to lead without arrogance, and to depend without fear. They understand that growth is not competition; it is cooperation. Like bananas ripening together, they discover that maturity is shared grace, not solitary achievement.

Reflection Questions

1. How intentional am I in nurturing the sense of belonging within my family? Do my children feel seen, heard, and valued?

2. Which "clusters" surround my child, family, Church, school, friendships, and how can I strengthen their positive influence?

3. Am I balancing boundaries with tenderness, giving my child both structure and warmth?

4. In what ways can I connect my family more deeply to the spiritual root, Christ, so that our cluster remains fruitful?

5. How can I model unity and forgiveness within my home so my children inherit peace, not division?

FRUIT OF THE WOMB

A Prayer of Blessing

Heavenly Father,

Thank you for designing us to grow together and not alone. I lift before You the children You have entrusted to my care. Let them be planted in the right clusters of family, faith, and community, where they will flourish in safety and love. Protect them from the loneliness and deception of isolation. Surround them with mentors and friends who reflect Your heart.

Help me, Lord, to lead my home as a faithful branch connected to Your Vine. Teach me to build unity, to speak gently, and to nurture patiently. May our household become a living bunch of grace, strong in love, steady in faith, and radiant in joy. I declare that my children will grow in wisdom and stature, in favor with God and man. Their lives will nourish others and testify to Your goodness. In Jesus' name, Amen.

FRUIT OF THE WOMB

Practical Family Activity – "Banana Bunch Night"

1. **Gather a Bunch:** Bring a full bunch of bananas to the table, unseparated. Observe how they grow together on one stalk.

2. **Family Discussion:** Explain that God designed us the same way, to belong to family, friends, and the Church.

3. **Togetherness Exercise:** Each family member takes one banana but stays seated close together while eating. Discuss how being connected keeps everyone strong and healthy.

4. **Gratitude List:** Invite each person to name one person outside the home (a teacher, friend, or church member) who strengthens them. Write those names as part of your "family cluster list."

5. **Prayer of Unity:** Close by joining hands and thanking God for every person who forms your cluster. Pray for unity, patience, and love to continue binding your family and community together.

Conclusion

The banana teaches a truth humanity often forgets: we were never meant to grow alone. Children who live in clusters of love and faith develop not only sweetness but stamina. Their innocence matures into integrity; their individuality blossoms within belonging.

Bananas hanging together are not just beautiful, they are balanced. Their collective weight distributes evenly, allowing each to ripen in peace. So too with families and churches rooted in Christ. When we grow together, we grow strong. When we remain connected, we stay fruitful.

Psalm 92:13 (KJV) says, *"Those that be planted in the house of the Lord shall flourish in the courts of our God."* Flourishing is never solitary; it is communal. Every child planted in God's orchard of grace becomes nourishment for generations.

The fruit of the womb, when raised in clusters of prayer, patience, and presence, becomes the fruit of the Kingdom, sweet to the taste, rich in unity, and full of life everlasting.

CHAPTER 4

THE GRAPES: CONNECTEDNESS AND LEGACY

Grapes tell the story of connection. They never grow alone. Instead, they form clusters, each grape drawing nourishment from the same Vine, growing side by side, sheltered under the same leaves. The design of the grape reveals God's divine blueprint for family, faith, and human flourishing. Life is meant to flow through connection.

Children, like grapes, are not created for isolation. From their first cry, they reach outward for arms that hold them, voices that soothe them, and hearts that recognize them. God designed childhood to unfold within a network of relationships—family, church, and community—because growth happens best where love and belonging intersect.

Jesus declared, *"I am the vine; you are the branches. Whoever lives in Me and I in him bears much fruit. However, apart from Me, you can do nothing"* (*John 15:5, AMP*). The Vine is Christ Himself, the source of all life. Parents, mentors, and communities serve as branches extending that life, shaping the environment in which children are nourished. When the Vine is strong and the branches healthy, the fruit thrives.

FRUIT OF THE WOMB

The beauty of grapes lies in their interdependence. Each one draws life not through isolation but through connection. *Ecclesiastes 4:9-10* affirms, *"Two are better than one, because they have a good return for their labor. If either of them falls down, one can help the other up"* (NIV). This simple truth resonates deeply with the developmental needs of children. They learn resilience not through detachment but through relationship. They grow strong not by separation but by support.

Yet modern life often fractures this design. Families eat separately, worship separately, and live under the same roof but rarely share the same rhythm. Technology connects us across distance but disconnects us across the dinner table. Many children today experience the ache of being surrounded yet unseen, connected online yet isolated in spirit.

Psalm 68:6 declares, *"God sets the lonely in families."* This verse reveals both God's intent and His intervention. Family is His chosen antidote to loneliness, the living cluster where children are meant to be rooted and restored. When children grow within the stability of loving homes, they learn emotional safety. When they belong to a community of faith, they learn spiritual identity.

In biblical imagery, the vineyard captures the heart of divine connectedness. *Isaiah 5:1–2* paints this picture: *"My loved one had a vineyard on a fertile hillside. He dug it up and cleared it of stones and planted it with the choicest vines."* God Himself models intentional cultivation. He clears, plants, and protects. Parents mirror this pattern when they create homes that nurture connection rather than competition, conversation rather than silence.

Connection does not simply happen; it must be cultivated. Just as a trellis must support a grapevine to grow upward, families must build spiritual and emotional structures that guide their children toward God. This "trellis" includes shared prayer, consistent affection, honest dialogue, and boundaries rooted in love. These elements lift the Vine from the ground, keeping it from decay and directing it toward light.

Jesus said, *"Remain in Me, and I will remain in you. No branch can bear fruit by itself; it must remain in the vine"* (*John 15:4, NIV*). To remain is to stay connected, to resist the drift of independence that cuts off life. Children mirror what they see. When parents model dependence on God, they teach their children to anchor their lives in Him.

Grapes also remind us that connection to the Vine brings collective strength. A single grape, detached, dries into a raisin. But in the cluster, it stays plump, vibrant, and full of juice. Similarly, a child detached from a spiritual community quickly dries up in purpose and joy; their faith withers when it is not reinforced by others who believe, worship, and grow together.

Deuteronomy 6:6-7 offers divine strategy for building this connectedness: *"These commandments that I give you today are to be on your hearts. Impress them on your children. Talk about them when you sit at home and when you walk along the road, when you lie down and when you get up"* (NIV). Connection is not built in grand moments but in daily rhythms—in conversations at mealtime, bedtime prayers, shared laughter, and mutual service.

The grapevine also warns of fragility. Grapes bruise easily; they must be handled with care. In the same way, children's hearts are tender. Words can wound as deeply as neglect. Paul urged, *"Fathers, do not embitter your children, or they will become discouraged"* (*Colossians 3:21, NIV*). To stay connected, love must be gentle. Firmness without compassion crushes; patience without presence weakens. God's design for family is not authoritarian rule but relational leadership—parents guiding from love, not fear.

Connectedness is not only emotional; it is spiritual. When children experience a parent's prayer over them, they learn intimacy with God. When they see forgiveness modeled after conflict, they understand grace. When they witness generosity toward others, they grasp kingdom living. Every act of love, every shared devotion, becomes a conduit through which divine life flows from the Vine into the next generation.

The vineyard is God's chosen picture of togetherness because fruitfulness is always collective. A single grape brings sweetness, but a cluster produces a harvest. A family bound in faith and love multiplies influence. A church that nurtures its children multiplies generations of disciples. *Ephesians 4:16* teaches, *"From Him the whole body, joined and held together by every supporting ligament, grows and builds itself up in love"* (NIV).

This is the secret of the grape. Unity strengthens life. Children who remain connected to God, to family, and to faith community grow into balanced, resilient adults. They are less likely to be crushed by the pressures of culture because their roots draw from divine supply. Parents who preserve connection create spiritual continuity, a lineage of grace that cannot be severed by distance or time.

To grow a child is to tend a vine. To strengthen a family is to nurture a vineyard. And when the branches remain in the Vine, the fruit will always be sweet, abundant, and enduring.

Cultivating Legacy — Generations That Endure

Every grape carries within it a small, hidden, yet potent seed with the power of generations. One grape may seem insignificant, but when its seed is planted, it holds the potential for entire vineyards yet unseen. In this same way, every child carries destiny and legacy. They are not merely born to fill the present; they are designed to extend the faith, values, and righteousness of their families into the future.

God revealed Himself not as *"the God of a man"* but as *"the God of Abraham, Isaac, and Jacob."* He identifies Himself through generational connection because His blessings are designed to move through lineage. *Psalm 112:2* declares, *"Their children will be mighty in the land; the generation of the upright will be blessed"* (NIV). Legacy is God's way of ensuring that truth does not end with one generation but continues to bear fruit in the next.

A grapevine lives for decades, sending out new shoots each year. Parents, too, are called to nurture spiritual branches that will outlive them. *Deuteronomy 6:6-7* provides divine strategy for legacy: *"These commandments that I give you today are to be on your hearts. Impress them on your children. Talk about them when you sit at home and when you walk along the road, when you lie down and when you get up"* (NIV). Legacy is not preserved through speeches or ceremonies but through consistent, everyday modeling of faith.

Each act of prayer with a child, each moment of forgiveness, and each time the family opens Scripture together becomes seedwork in the soil of legacy. Parents are gardeners of generational vineyards. Their role is not only to raise children who succeed in the world but to cultivate heirs who sustain the kingdom. *Proverbs 17:6* says, *"Children's children are a crown to the aged, and parents are the pride of their children"* (NIV). When parents live faithfully, they plant memories that become moral anchors for future generations.

However, legacy does not happen by sentiment; it requires cultivation. In every vineyard, pruning is essential. Jesus taught, *"Every branch that does bear fruit He prunes, that it may bear more fruit"* (*John 15:2, ESV*). Parents participate in this process when they guide, correct, and discipline with love. Pruning is never punishment; it is purposeful refinement. It removes the distractions that compete with destiny and focuses growth on fruit that lasts.

The absence of pruning, however, leads to overgrowth, a life full of activity but lacking in purpose. In the same way, children who are given freedom without guidance often grow wild and fruitless. Loving correction, balanced with affirmation, trims away attitudes and behaviors that hinder destiny. It teaches accountability while preserving self-worth. *"No discipline seems pleasant at the time, but painful,"* writes the author of Hebrews, *"but later it yields the peaceful fruit of righteousness to those who have been trained by it"* (*Hebrews 12:11, ESV*).

Legacy also demands remembrance. Just as vineyards are passed from one generation to another, so too must stories, testimonies, and faith experiences be preserved.

When parents share how God answered prayer, provided in hardship, or guided their family through trial, they pass down more than information—they transmit faith DNA. *Psalm 145:4* affirms, *"One generation shall commend your works to another, and shall declare your mighty acts"* (ESV).

But legacy can also be lost. *Judges 2:10* gives a solemn warning: *"After that whole generation had been gathered to their ancestors, another generation grew up who knew neither the Lord nor what he had done for Israel"* (NIV).

The vineyard of faith must never be left untended. Disconnection from spiritual heritage leads to decay. Parents must, therefore, intentionally weave God's truth into family culture, not as religion but as rhythm.

Just as grapes are transformed when pressed, legacy often matures through pressure. Crushing seasons produce richness that sweetness alone cannot achieve. When families endure hardship together and continue to trust God, they produce *wine* — the deep joy and maturity that only come from faith tested by time. *Romans 12:2* calls believers to transformation: *"Do not be conformed to this world, but be transformed by the renewing of your mind"* (NRSV). Transformation is the process by which ordinary faith becomes an enduring legacy.

Legacy-minded parents look beyond immediate results. They understand that the fruit of their labor may ripen long after they are gone. Like a vintner planting vines he may never harvest, they labor in hope.

Galatians 6:9 encourages, *"Let us not become weary in doing good, for at the proper time we will reap a harvest if we do not give up"* (NIV). True legacy is not measured by fame or fortune but by the faithfulness that multiplies in the lives of one's children and grandchildren.

The beauty of the grape teaches us that destiny is not solitary. The seeds we sow today will germinate in the souls of tomorrow's children. When we train them to stay connected to the Vine, we ensure that the vineyard of God's kingdom continues to flourish across generations.

The Joy and Strength of the Cluster — Community, Pruning, and Fruitfulness

No vineyard flourishes under one gardener alone. The tending of vines requires a team, workers who water, prune, support, and gather. Parenting mirrors this principle. God designed families to thrive in community, not isolation. Parents, mentors, teachers, and church leaders together form the *vineyard crew* that helps children grow toward purpose.

The proverb remains true: *"As iron sharpens iron, so one person sharpens another"* (*Proverbs 27:17, NIV*). Children learn through imitation and interaction. Their social worlds—family, friends, and faith communities—serve as the environment where character is shaped. In the cluster of community, they discover empathy, cooperation, and accountability. When one child stumbles, others help restore; when one rejoices, others celebrate. That is the rhythm of connected growth.

Healthy clusters also provide protection. A grape surrounded by others is less likely to wither. Similarly, children in loving environments are shielded from many emotional and spiritual predators. The family's prayers act as nets; the church's teaching forms the trellis; the community's shared faith becomes the soil that nourishes. *Proverbs 11:14* teaches, *"Where there is no guidance, a nation falls, but in an abundance of counselors there is safety"* (ESV). The safety of many voices grounded in truth keeps children steady when temptations arise.

FRUIT OF THE WOMB

In every cluster, however, tension exists. Grapes press against one another; leaves compete for sunlight; branches intertwine. Family life is no different. Growth brings friction—disagreements, differing temperaments, conflicting goals. But within that friction, God forges maturity. The same pressure that could crush can also create strength when handled with grace. Unity does not mean uniformity; it means harmony through love. *Psalm 133:1* celebrates this truth: *"How good and pleasant it is when God's people live together in unity!"* (NIV).

Children learn this harmony through modeling. When parents disagree respectfully, reconcile quickly, and express forgiveness, they demonstrate what covenant love looks like. The cluster stays intact, not because it is perfect, but because it remains connected. The strength of any cluster lies in its ability to hold together even under strain.

Pruning continues to play a crucial role in this communal strength. It is not only individuals who need correction but family systems as a whole. Families must periodically examine habits, priorities, and cultural influences to ensure that nothing is choking the life of the Vine. Activities that crowd out prayer, media that diminish faith, or schedules that erode family time are all shoots that must be trimmed. Pruning is not loss; it is alignment.

Emotional and spiritual resilience also emerge within clusters. When one family member grows weary, another can lend encouragement. When a child faces a challenge—an academic struggle, a social disappointment, or a moral test—the family's unity becomes a cushion. The cluster absorbs the pressure. *"Bear one another's burdens, and so fulfill the law of Christ,"* Paul writes in *Galatians 6:2 (ESV)*. In a community, burdens are lighter because they are shared.

Fruitfulness, then, is the outcome of unity and care. A cluster ripens together. Parents who remain steadfast in love and faith eventually see maturity blossom in their children's lives. The sweet taste of the harvest appears in moments when children make wise choices, show compassion, or demonstrate faithfulness without being prompted. These are the grapes of joy that reward years of labor.

Psalm 126:5-6 speaks hope to every weary parent: *"Those who sow in tears shall reap with shouts of joy. He who goes out weeping, bearing the seed for sowing, shall come home with shouts of joy, bringing his sheaves with him"* (ESV). What feels hidden in sowing will one day be revealed in harvest. No prayer over a child is wasted; no tear shed in intercession goes unnoticed. In due season, God ripens every promise.

FRUIT OF THE WOMB

The final beauty of the grape is transformation. Grapes are not only consumed as fruit; they are pressed into juice and wine that bring refreshment and joy. This pressing process reflects the refining work of God in children's lives. Trials, discipline, and seasons of waiting are the vineyard's press—producing endurance and depth. Under divine pressure, raw potential becomes mature purpose.

As children grow within clusters of faith, they become vessels of renewal. They refresh families, strengthen churches, and bless societies. Their connectedness produces compassion; their pruning yields wisdom; their unity bears testimony to God's sustaining grace. When generations remain joined to the Vine and to each other, the fruit of the womb becomes nourishment for nations.

FRUIT OF THE WOMB

Reflection Questions

1. In what ways am I helping my child stay connected to Christ, the true Vine?

2. How intentionally do I cultivate generational legacy through prayer, conversation, and shared faith practices?

3. Are there habits or influences in our home that need pruning so that greater fruitfulness can emerge?

4. How can I strengthen the cluster of community around my child, family, mentors, and church?

5. What "harvest fruit" do I already see in my children, and how can I celebrate it as part of God's ongoing work?

A Prayer of Blessing

Father, thank You for designing our families like vineyards where life flows from connection and generations are nourished by Your love. Keep my children firmly attached to You, the true Vine. Teach me to prune wisely, to guide patiently, and to sow faithfully. Let my home become a fruitful vineyard where grace and truth thrive. May the seeds in my children mature into legacies that bless others. Strengthen our family cluster so that we remain united through every season and resilient in every storm. Let our fruit endure for generations and bring glory to Your name.

In Jesus' name, Amen.

Practical Family Activity – *Vineyard Legacy Night*

1. Purchase a cluster of grapes and keep them on the stem.

2. Show your children how each grape depends on the Vine for life. Explain: *"This is how we stay connected to Jesus and to one another."*

3. As the family eats the grapes together, have each person share one way they feel connected to the family and one way they can strengthen that bond.

4. Parents share a story of God's faithfulness or a family value that has shaped their lives.

5. End by praying together, thanking God for your *family vineyard*, and asking Him to keep every grape connected and fruitful.

CHAPTER 5

THE WATERMELON: HIDDEN RICHES WITHIN

Few fruits embody surprise quite like the watermelon. From the outside, it appears ordinary, a green shell marked by stripes or mottled shades of light and dark, often large and heavy, rolling awkwardly on the ground. Its exterior gives little hint of what lies inside. Yet once it is opened, the watermelon reveals a world of sweetness, vibrant red flesh, bursting with juice and flavor, full of seeds and life.

Children are much like this fruit. At first glance, they may seem simple or even unremarkable. But within every child lies a treasury of potential waiting to be discovered. Their true value cannot be measured by what meets the eye. God has hidden wisdom, creativity, faith, and purpose within each one, treasures that require patient discovery and gentle opening.

Psalm 139:16 (NIV) declares, "Your eyes saw my unformed body; all the days ordained for me were written in your book before one of them came to be." Before a child ever takes a breath, God has already written their story. He knows the sweetness inside even before the world does. Parents and mentors must learn to see children through this divine lens, not as they are, but as God has ordained them to be.

The watermelon's tough outer rind mirrors the unseen layers of a child's soul. On the surface, you may encounter shyness, rebellion, insecurity, or silence. But beneath those layers are treasures of tenderness, faith, and potential. The outer rind is not a flaw; it is a protective layer that guards what is still forming. A wise parent understands that a quiet child is not empty, and a talkative one is not shallow; both are filled with divine ingredients waiting to be drawn out through love, structure, and encouragement.

This is why 1 Samuel 16:7 (NIV) remains one of the most powerful principles for parenting: "The Lord does not look at the things people look at. People look at the outward appearance, but the Lord looks at the heart." Samuel's mistake in overlooking David is one that parents often make. Jesse's older sons looked like kings, tall, confident, impressive, but David, the overlooked shepherd boy, carried the sweetness of destiny. The fruit of his life was still hidden, waiting to be revealed at the right time.

So, it is with children. Some display their gifts early, others ripen later. But hidden potential is still potential. The outer rind of immaturity, awkwardness, or even failure does not define a child's fruitfulness. What matters most is what God has placed within.

FRUIT OF THE WOMB

Like a farmer who cuts open a watermelon to reveal its color and taste, parents are called to open their children, not through pressure or punishment, but through patient discovery. Proverbs 20:5 (AMP) reminds us, "Counsel in the heart of man is like water in a deep well, but a man of understanding draws it out." Inside every child is a deep well of insight, imagination, and calling. Parents who understand draw out those waters by listening, observing, and nurturing.

Consider the mystery of the watermelon's development. It begins as a seed buried in the soil, unseen and forgotten. Days pass with no visible progress, yet within that dark space, life stirs. The seed breaks open; roots form, vines stretch, blossoms bloom — all leading to fruit that was invisible at first. The same is true of a child's growth. God's purposes unfold quietly, often beneath the surface of what parents can see. The calling on their life may not bloom until adolescence, adulthood, or even beyond. Patience becomes an act of faith, trusting that what God has planted will emerge in due season.

Galatians 6:9 (NLT) encourages us, "Let's not get tired of doing what is good. At just the right time, we will reap a harvest of blessing if we don't give up." Parenting is often the art of waiting, trusting the hidden process. The sweetest fruit takes time to mature.

When you cut a watermelon, the first slice is often the most revealing moment, the unveiling of color, fragrance, and flavor. In the same way, there are moments in a child's life when God allows what has been hidden to be revealed, a word of wisdom spoken in innocence, a talent unexpectedly displayed, a compassionate act that reveals the heart. Each of these is a glimpse into the sweetness inside. Parents who remain attentive and prayerful will recognize these moments and nurture them rather than overlook them.

The world often values speed and appearance, but God values depth and timing. A watermelon ripened too soon is tasteless; a child forced into premature performance may become anxious or burnt out. Just as fruit must mature on the vine, children must grow under grace, in safety, love, and faith. The goal is not to expose them quickly but to develop them deeply.

David was not thrust into kingship overnight. Moses was not revealed as a deliverer until after decades of obscurity. Even Jesus "grew in wisdom and stature, and in favor with God and man" (Luke 2:52, NIV). God hides greatness within maturity. The rind is not rejection; it is protection.

Parents are therefore called to adopt God's pace. They are gardeners, not sculptors. Their task is not to shape the fruit according to personal preference but to cultivate an environment where divine potential can flourish. This means choosing words that heal rather than wound, offering discipline that guides rather than shames, and creating spaces where a child's curiosity can bloom freely.

Children are more than their grades, behaviors, or appearances. They are vessels of divine creativity and promise, hidden watermelons in the field of humanity. A parent who learns to see past the rind participates in one of the greatest acts of faith: believing in what God has placed within before it is visible to anyone else.

The watermelon, then, becomes a symbol of divine mystery. It reminds us that every child carries more within than meets the eye. The sweetness is there, hidden, waiting, protected by the very layers that frustrate us. The task of the faithful parent is to keep nurturing, keep believing, and when the time is right, to help reveal the hidden riches God has placed inside.

Seeds of Potential – Cultivating What Lies Within

When the watermelon is opened, its sweetness is not the only discovery. Embedded within its flesh are hundreds of seeds, small and dark, easily dismissed yet full of life. Many people remove or spit out these seeds without realizing that they carry the power to reproduce an entire field of fruit. What looks insignificant is, in truth, the key to multiplication.

FRUIT OF THE WOMB

Children are just like this. Their lives are filled with small, seemingly unimportant moments, questions, curiosities, and ideas that may appear trivial but are actually the seeds of future greatness. Every interest they express, every skill they attempt, every dream they whisper could be the seed of destiny.

The challenge for parents and communities is to recognize those seeds early and nurture them wisely. Too often, adults try to control or suppress them because they do not fit expectations. But the calling of godly parenting is not to decide which seeds deserve to grow; it is to create the conditions for every seed to have a chance to sprout.

Zechariah 8:5 (NIV) offers a beautiful image of flourishing: *"The city streets will be filled with boys and girls playing there."* The laughter of children represents more than joy; it represents potential. Their energy is a prophetic sign of renewal. When children play, imagine, and create, they are already rehearsing for the roles God has ordained for them.

Parents are called to observe the seeds without judgment. A child who loves to dance may carry the seed of worship or artistry. One who constantly fixes broken objects may possess the seed of innovation. Another who speaks words of comfort to others may hold the seed of ministry. None of these gifts are fully developed yet; they are seeds that need the sunlight of encouragement and the water of affirmation.

Isaiah 45:3 (NLT) reminds us that *"God gives hidden treasures, riches stored in secret places."* Those treasures are often stored in children's hearts, sometimes buried beneath layers of fear, insecurity, or shyness. Parents must draw them out through love, exposure, and opportunity. The role of the parent is not to push but to pull out, to make space for what God has planted to emerge naturally.

Seeds also require protection. The rind of the watermelon shields its contents from harsh sun, insects, and decay until it reaches maturity. Likewise, parents must guard their children's gifts from premature exposure. Some talents must be nurtured in private before they are displayed in public. Joseph's youthful dreams were true, but sharing them too early brought him unnecessary rejection and pain (*Genesis 37*). Protection is not suppression; it is stewardship.

This protective covering also includes setting boundaries, moral, emotional, and spiritual, that preserve the purity of the heart. A seed exposed to too much sun withers; a child exposed to too much worldliness too soon can lose their sweetness. Parents serve as the *rind* that shields the child from pressures that might distort their purpose before maturity.

Finally, seeds remind us of legacy. One watermelon contains enough seeds to plant a garden. Similarly, one child carries within them the capacity to influence generations. Every child is a seed-bearer, not only for their own destiny but for others. A child taught to love God can raise another generation that fears Him. A young person inspired toward service can ignite compassion in an entire community.

The watermelon's many seeds whisper this truth: inside every child are possibilities beyond counting. The role of the parent is to cherish each one, nurture them with prayer, and wait patiently for God's timing to bring forth fruit in abundance.

The Refreshing Fruit – Joy, Revelation, and Legacy

When the watermelon is finally opened, it becomes a symbol of joy and refreshment. It is rarely eaten in solitude; instead, it appears at family gatherings, picnics, and celebrations. Its sweetness is meant to be shared. This imagery speaks powerfully to the purpose of every child's hidden riches. They are not designed for private enjoyment alone but to refresh families, communities, and even nations.

Zechariah 8:5 gives us a prophetic glimpse of this: *"The city streets will be filled with boys and girls playing there."* In God's kingdom, the sound of children laughing is not a distraction; it is evidence of blessing. Their presence, their play, their creativity all announce that life and hope have returned to the land. Just as watermelon quenches thirst on a summer day, children refresh the weary world through their joy, imagination, and innocence.

Every parent knows that a child's laughter can change the atmosphere of a home. It brings warmth to the discouraged, light to the weary, and peace to those burdened by care. Jesus Himself valued the refreshing purity of children, declaring in *Matthew 18:3 (NLT)*, *"Unless you turn from your sins and become like little children, you will never get into the Kingdom of Heaven."* Children carry a kingdom quality, unfiltered faith, trust, and delight. They remind us of God's own joy and of the simplicity of love.

Yet, just as watermelon must be protected until harvest, so must children's joy be safeguarded. In a world of busyness, technology, and comparison, the sweetness of childhood can easily be lost. Many homes are filled with activity but empty of connection. Parents, therefore, have a divine responsibility to create rhythms of rest, laughter, and conversation that keep the fruit from drying out.

Psalm 127:3 (KJV) reminds us, *"Children are an heritage of the Lord: and the fruit of the womb is his reward."* They are not burdens to be managed but rewards to be enjoyed. Each day with them is an invitation to taste the sweetness of God's grace afresh. Their laughter is a melody of divine generosity.

But watermelon does more than refresh; it also nourishes. It replenishes what heat and exhaustion have drained away. Likewise, children possess the ability to renew vision in adults. They remind us of what it means to believe again, to dream again, and to love without condition. Parents often discover, through their children, forgotten parts of themselves: compassion, patience, playfulness, and faith. God uses children to sanctify adults, peeling back layers of selfishness and awakening tenderness once lost.

Proverbs 23:24 (NIV) declares, *"The father of a righteous child has great joy; a man who fathers a wise son rejoices in him."* Joy is the natural harvest of faithful parenting. When a parent witnesses their child walking in wisdom, the sweetness surpasses every previous sacrifice. Each lesson, each prayer, each night of worry gives way to songs of rejoicing when fruit begins to show.

The watermelon also teaches us about revelation, the act of uncovering what God has hidden. No one can enjoy the sweetness until the fruit is opened. In the same way, hidden treasures within children remain inaccessible until parents, mentors, and spiritual communities take deliberate action to *open* them through prayer, guidance, and affirmation. *Proverbs 25:2 (AMP)* states, *"It is the glory of God to conceal a matter, but the glory of kings is to search out a matter."* Parenting becomes a royal act when we seek out the divine mysteries God has concealed in our children.

However, revelation without preservation leads to waste. A watermelon, once opened, must be devoured or refrigerated; otherwise, it spoils. Similarly, once a child's gifts are revealed, they must be stewarded. Discovery must be followed by discipleship. Parents must help children channel their abilities toward a godly purpose, teaching humility, gratitude, and service. A gift that is not rooted in God's character can easily become corrupted by pride or misuse.

This is why Jesus said in *John 15:5 (NIV)*, *"I am the Vine; you are the branches. If you remain in me and I in you, you will bear much fruit; apart from me you can do nothing."* The greatest treasure within a child is not their skill or intellect, but their capacity to remain connected to Christ, the true Vine. Every other fruit flows from that relationship.

Finally, the watermelon points us toward legacy. Within every slice are seeds, each one capable of producing future harvests. Parents who uncover their children's gifts are not simply shaping one life; they are influencing generations to come. The impact of a nurtured child extends far beyond the present.

A mother's prayer, a father's blessing, a teacher's encouragement, these are the tools that plant seeds of greatness for future seasons. Abraham could not see the full harvest of his obedience. Still, God promised that his descendants would be as numerous as the stars (*Genesis 22:17*). In the same way, parents may not witness the whole fruit of their labor in their lifetime, but their faithfulness ensures that sweetness continues for generations.

One watermelon contains dozens of seeds. One family walking in faith can influence hundreds of lives. The fruit of the womb, when nurtured under God's hand, becomes nourishment for the world, not just for a season, but for eternity.

FRUIT OF THE WOMB

Reflection Questions

1. What hidden gifts or potentials have I noticed in my child that may not yet be fully revealed?

2. How can I provide opportunities for discovery without rushing or pressuring them?

3. Do I sometimes undervalue my child by focusing only on outward performance rather than inward treasures?

4. What protective *rind,* boundaries, prayers, or disciplines do I need to strengthen around my child to guard their potential?

5. How can I encourage my child to see their gifts as blessings for others, not just for themselves?

A Prayer of Blessing

Heavenly Father, thank You for the hidden treasures You have placed within my children. Help me to see beyond the surface and recognize the sweetness and potential you have woven into their lives. Give me wisdom to protect their gifts, patience to wait for Your timing, and faith to nurture what I cannot yet see. Teach me to open their hearts gently, drawing out the beauty You have placed inside. May their lives refresh others like cool water on a hot day, and may their hidden riches bless families, communities, and nations for generations to come. *In Jesus' name, Amen.*

Practical Family Activity – "Watermelon Treasure Night"

1. **Prepare together:** Cut open a watermelon in front of the family. Before tasting, ask the children to describe what they expected to see inside.

2. **Teach the lesson:** Explain, *"Sometimes people cannot see the treasure God has placed inside us. But just like this watermelon, God has hidden sweetness and seeds of greatness within you."*

3. **Share and reflect:** Invite each child to share one hidden dream, gift, or idea they have. Parents record these in a *Family Treasure Journal.*

4. **Pray together:** As you eat, pray over each dream, asking God to protect and nurture it.

5. **Plant a seed:** Save a few watermelon seeds and plant them in soil as a family reminder that treasures grow when watered with love, patience, and prayer.

CHAPTER 6

THE CHERRY – SMALL BUT PRECIOUS

Among all fruits, the cherry stands out not for its size but for its brilliance. Tiny, glossy, and full of vibrant color, it captures attention not through grandeur but through grace. Cherries are brief visitors to the market, appearing for only a short season each year, and that may be part of their allure. They remind us that what is fleeting can also be priceless.

Children, in much the same way, mirror the cherry. Their smallness does not diminish their value; it enhances it. Their short seasons of childhood, their tender voices, their wide-eyed wonder, all of these are treasures that pass quickly but leave eternal imprints. Jesus made this truth unmistakably clear in *Matthew 18:10:* "See that you do not despise one of these little ones. For I tell you that their angels in heaven always see the face of my Father in heaven."

The cherry's worth lies not in its quantity but in its quality, concentrated sweetness in a small package. Likewise, a child's impact cannot be measured by stature or speech. Within every small body lies a large destiny, wrapped in divine purpose. *God often places His greatest treasures in the smallest vessels.*

FRUIT OF THE WOMB

In a world that prizes size, performance, and visibility, God calls us to a countercultural perspective: *"The kingdom of heaven belongs to such as these" (Matthew 19:14).* Jesus not only blessed children; He used them as living parables. Their innocence, faith, and humility embodied the essence of His kingdom. Parents who recognize this truth become co-laborers with God in shaping souls that reflect heaven.

Smallness, in God's economy, has never been a limitation. The cherry may be small, but its sweetness is concentrated. A mustard seed may be tiny, yet Jesus said it could move mountains. A child may seem insignificant, yet their prayers can shift the spiritual atmosphere of a home. *To despise smallness is to misunderstand how God works.*

The culture of Jesus' time often dismissed children as irrelevant until adulthood. Yet He disrupted that thinking by placing a child at the center of His teaching, declaring, *"Unless you change and become like little children, you will never enter the kingdom of heaven" (Matthew 18:3).* He transformed the smallest into the standard, the least into the example, and the dependent into the model of true greatness.

For parents, this means learning to see value not through scale but through significance. Each word of affection, each moment of play, each bedtime story, and each prayer whispered over a sleeping child, these are *cherries of the soul:* small, sweet, and sacred.

2. The Fragile Season: Handling Hearts with Tenderness

The cherry's beauty is matched by its fragility. Its smooth, delicate skin bruises easily; rough handling destroys its perfection. The same is true of children's hearts. They may appear resilient, but inside, they are tender and impressionable. What touches them deeply can shape their identity for years to come.

Proverbs 18:21 teaches, "The tongue has the power of life and death, and those who love it will eat its fruit." The words spoken to and about children either nourish or wound their spirits. Encouragement, affirmation, and prayer strengthen their confidence; criticism, neglect, or harshness leave bruises that may not heal easily. Parents must learn to speak with care, for *words are like hands; they can either cradle or crush.*

To handle cherries properly, one must wash them gently, store them carefully, and savor them slowly. The same principles apply to parenting. Children must be cleansed through consistent love, stored within safe emotional environments, and savored for who they are rather than rushed into who we want them to be. Childhood is a fragile but sacred window of time, a brief season meant to be enjoyed, not hurried.

Psalm 90:12 calls us to wisdom: "Teach us to number our days, that we may gain a heart of wisdom." Parents must learn to number the days of their children's youth, understanding that seasons of play, curiosity, and dependence pass quickly. The "cherry years" of parenting, those short, sweet years of childlike laughter and endless questions, must be cherished.

Just as cherries bruise from rough handling, children bruise from neglect. Ignoring their emotional needs, dismissing their questions, or belittling their feelings leaves silent wounds. Parents must remember that even discipline can be delivered with dignity. *Correction is not rejection.* The goal of discipline is restoration, not humiliation.

Tenderness does not mean weakness; it means wisdom. Even God, in His dealings with His people, reveals Himself as both firm and gentle. *Psalm 103:13* declares, "As a father has compassion on his children, so the Lord has compassion on those who fear him." Compassion, not control, is the essence of divine parenting.

Every cherry also holds a pit, a firm center that protects its seed. Likewise, every child carries an inner core of identity that must be safeguarded. Within that pit lies their God-given spirit and destiny.

FRUIT OF THE WOMB

Ecclesiastes 3:11 says, "He has also set eternity in the human heart." Even from early childhood, children possess an awareness of meaning and belonging that points back to their Creator.

Parents are entrusted to protect that inner core, to guard their child's spirit from comparison, shame, and worldly distortion. A child who is constantly compared to others may begin to doubt their worth. But when parents affirm their uniqueness, saying, *"You are exactly who God made you to be,"* they strengthen the core from which resilience grows.

Tender care involves both physical presence and emotional attunement. It is not enough to provide food and shelter; children thrive on connection, eye contact, affirmation, and spiritual covering. Every moment of kindness plants seeds of confidence. Every prayer whispered over them waters the soil of their destiny.

Cherries must be picked at the right time, not too early, or they will be sour; not too late, or they will spoil. Likewise, children must be guided in season. There is a time to shelter and a time to stretch; a time to correct and a time to celebrate; a time to hold close and a time to release. *Wisdom is knowing the difference.*

Isaiah 40:11 paints a tender portrait of God's shepherding heart: "He tends his flock like a shepherd: He gathers the lambs in his arms and carries them close to his heart; he gently leads those that have young." God Himself models the rhythm of nurture and guidance that parents must emulate, leading gently, guarding diligently, and loving constantly.

To handle children as cherries is to remember: *they are tender but resilient, petite but eternal, and momentary yet priceless.* The fruit may be seasonal, but the seeds within are forever.

3. The Power of Smallness: Joy, Legacy, and Divine Reward

Smallness is God's secret strategy. Throughout Scripture, He consistently uses what is little to accomplish what is large. He delights in reversing human expectations, using a shepherd to defeat a giant, a widow's mite to shame the wealthy, and a child's lunch to feed thousands. The cherry, small yet bursting with sweetness, stands as a symbol of how God packages greatness within what the world deems insignificant.

Children embody this divine paradox. They are small in stature, yet vast in potential; fragile in body, yet powerful in spirit. Their voices may seem soft, but in God's ear, they are mighty. *Psalm 8:2* declares, "Through the praise of children and infants you have established a stronghold against your enemies, to silence the foe and the avenger." In other words, children's worship carries authority. Their laughter and prayers are not noise but spiritual weapons that shift atmospheres and silence opposition.

When parents nurture their children's spiritual lives, they participate in divine warfare. Every bedtime prayer, every moment of worship, and every act of faith sown in a young heart strengthens the walls of the household. The *cherry principle* reminds us that small things, when blessed by God, carry eternal weight.

Small but Spiritually Significant

Children often understand God in ways that adults complicate. Their faith is uncluttered, their worship unpretentious, and their obedience swift. Jesus praised this kind of simplicity when He said, *"I praise you, Father, because you have hidden these things from the wise and learned, and revealed them to little children"* (Matthew 11:25).

This means that the smallest believers can often grasp the most significant truths. Parents must never assume that children are too young to encounter God. Samuel, still a boy, heard God's voice in the night. The child prophet's simple response, *"Speak, Lord, for your servant is listening,"* reshaped a nation. Josiah, crowned king at eight, led a revival. The boy who shared his lunch became part of a miracle that fed multitudes.

Each of these stories demonstrates the same truth: children are not the future church; they are the church now. They are not spiritual apprentices waiting to grow into usefulness; they are vessels of divine purpose already at work. Parents who cultivate prayer, worship, and service in their children are equipping the next generation of reformers, leaders, and intercessors.

Paul's words to Timothy echo through time: *"Don't let anyone look down on you because you are young, but set an example for the believers in speech, in conduct, in love, in faith and in purity"* (1 Timothy 4:12). This is God's challenge to both the young and those who raise them, to recognize that size does not determine strength, and youth does not diminish calling.

Children are cherries in God's hand, small yet filled with sweetness, fleeting yet eternally impactful. Their prayers shake heaven, their songs carry purity untainted by pride, and their faith moves mountains that adults rationalize as immovable. Parents must learn to stand in awe of their children's spiritual capacity.

Fragility and Resilience: The Paradox of the Pit

Every cherry, for all its softness, contains a hard, immovable pit at its core. This inner stone represents resilience, the strength to endure, and the capacity to reproduce. Likewise, children, though outwardly fragile, possess remarkable resilience. Life may bruise them, but within their spirits lies divine strength that can outlast hardship.

Isaiah 40: 29–31 captures this beautifully: *"He gives strength to the weary and increases the power of the weak. Even youths grow tired and weary, and young men stumble and fall, but those who hope in the Lord will renew their strength."* Though children depend on adults for protection, they carry within them an extraordinary ability to recover, adapt, and grow.

Consider how children often mirror God's heart through forgiveness. A child wronged in the morning may embrace the offender by evening. Their hearts, though tender, rebound quickly when met with love and assurance. This resilience is divine design, proof that God built them not merely to survive but to thrive through grace.

Parents are called to guard this inner pit of strength, to teach children how to draw power from God's Spirit rather than from performance or popularity. True resilience is not self-reliance; it is God-reliance. When children learn early that their identity and value rest in being loved by God, they develop an unshakable core that withstands the storms of adolescence and adulthood.

This is why spiritual formation must begin early. Teaching children Scripture, prayer, and gratitude fortifies the pit of their being. It builds a moral and spiritual backbone capable of resisting cultural decay. *Ephesians 6:4* gives this charge: *"Bring them up in the training and instruction of the Lord."* Parents who do this are not simply raising good children; they are shaping durable souls that can carry faith into generations.

Fragility without cultivation leads to bruising; resilience without grounding leads to pride. But when both are held in balance, tenderness and toughness, innocence and instruction, a child becomes a living testimony of grace. Like a cherry that withstands sun and rain yet retains sweetness, a well-nurtured child grows resilient without losing purity.

Generational Joy and Legacy

Cherries are fruits of celebration. Their bright red hue and burst of sweetness symbolize joy, festivity, and fullness. In the same way, children fill homes with laughter, delight, and divine reward. *Proverbs 17:6* rejoices, *"Children's children are a crown to the aged, and parents are the pride of their children."* A child's smile is not merely sentimental; it is sacramental. It reminds families that God is still creating, still blessing, and still continuing His covenant of life.

Parents who learn to savor the cherry seasons of life, those brief, precious years of growth and innocence, receive a double blessing: joy in the present and legacy for the future. Each giggle, each milestone, each bedtime prayer becomes a seed sown into eternity. Childhood passes quickly, but its impact echoes for generations.

The cherry's short season teaches us to slow down and savor. Many parents, overwhelmed by schedules and ambitions, unintentionally rush through their children's most formative years. Yet the Word calls us to pause. *Psalm 127:3–4* reminds us, *"Children are a heritage from the Lord, offspring a reward from him. Like arrows in the hands of a warrior are children born in one's youth."* A heritage must be cherished; a reward must be received with gratitude, not exhaustion.

When families intentionally celebrate smallness, the first prayer, the first verse memorized, the first act of kindness, they multiply joy. These are the cherries of family legacy: small but cumulative, sweet but sustaining. The joy that begins in one generation spills into the next.

Deuteronomy 6: 6–7 commands, *"These commandments that I give you today are to be on your hearts. Impress them on your children. Talk about them when you sit at home and when you walk along the road, when you lie down and when you get up."* This verse paints a picture of faith not as a formal lecture but as a lifestyle. Legacy is not built in grand gestures but in daily conversations, shared meals, and unhurried moments.

Joy becomes a legacy when faith is lived, not just taught. When a child sees love expressed between parents, kindness practiced toward strangers, and worship made a family rhythm, they internalize those patterns. Like cherries ripening on a shared stem, family members mature together in joy and grace.

Smallness as God's Pathway to Greatness

The cherry concludes with a final revelation: God does His greatest work through what seems least. The Savior of the world came not as a conqueror but as a baby. The redemption of humanity began not with thunder but with a child's cry. God's plan has always favored humility over grandeur.

Zechariah 4:10 asks, *"Who dares despise the day of small things?"* The question remains for every parent: who dares despise the day of small voices, small prayers, small hands clasped in faith? To despise smallness is to miss God's method. Every great movement begins with something, or someone, small.

The cherry reminds us that divine sweetness is concentrated, not diluted. God compresses His glory into humble vessels. Children, with their laughter and trust, become living testimonies that the kingdom of God still advances through purity and simplicity. Parents who honor that smallness partner with heaven in its most sacred work, shaping eternal souls.

FRUIT OF THE WOMB

When a child's potential is nurtured, their spirit blossoms. When their small victories are celebrated, their confidence soars. When their faith is affirmed, their destiny unfolds. Every cherry-sized act of faith, a whispered prayer, a kind gesture, a word of gratitude, becomes fruit that heaven counts as abundance.

FRUIT OF THE WOMB

Reflection Questions

1. Do I recognize the divine value in the small moments of my child's life, or do I rush past them in busyness?

2. How can I nurture both my child's tenderness and resilience, protecting their fragility while strengthening their inner core?

3. In what ways am I helping my child experience God personally, not just hear about Him?

4. Do I celebrate the small victories and moments of joy that form our family legacy?

5. How might I align my parenting with God's strategy of using smallness to accomplish greatness?

FRUIT OF THE WOMB

A Prayer of Blessing

Father, thank You for the precious gift of children, small in size yet vast in worth. Teach me to cherish every moment, to handle their hearts with tenderness, and to see the eternal significance hidden in their simplicity. Help me to speak life, to model faith, and to celebrate joy in every season. Strengthen their inner core with Your Spirit, and let their smallness reveal Your greatness. May their laughter fill our home with light, and their faith become a legacy that endures for generations. In Jesus' name, Amen.

Practical Family Activity: "Cherry Moments"

Step 1: Share a bowl of cherries or another small fruit. Invite the family to eat slowly, savoring the sweetness.

Step 2: Explain, "Cherries are small, but they are precious and full of joy. Childhood is like this, short but beautiful."

Step 3: Invite children to recall their favorite small joys from the week. Parents affirm each as a *cherry moment* worth remembering.

Step 4: Each parent shares one trait or gift they see developing in their child, something small now but full of future promise.

FRUIT OF THE WOMB

Step 5: End the night in prayer, thanking God for every *cherry moment* of family life and asking for grace to savor and protect these fleeting seasons

CHAPTER 7

THE PINEAPPLE: STRENGTH AND SWEETNESS

The pineapple is one of the most fascinating fruits in creation. With its spiky armor, rough rind, and bold crown, it commands attention long before it is tasted. Its hard exterior seems to warn away the casual touch, but inside lies something completely different. The golden flesh is juicy, fragrant, and sweet. Its ruggedness conceals tenderness, and its toughness protects treasure. This balance between strength and sweetness makes the pineapple a vivid metaphor for children.

Children, like pineapples, often appear one way on the surface but hold something entirely different within. They may seem stubborn, defiant, or overly independent, but beneath those layers are hearts soft with longing, curiosity, and love. What appears as resistance is sometimes the only language a child has to communicate vulnerability. Parents and mentors who understand this truth learn to look beyond behavior and see the need beneath it. God, after all, looks past appearances. *"Man looks at the outward appearance, but the Lord looks at the heart"* (1 Samuel 16:7, NIV). Every child has a golden center, but reaching it requires insight and patience.

FRUIT OF THE WOMB

The outer skin of the pineapple was designed to withstand the sun, storms, and handling. It keeps insects out and moisture in until the fruit is ready for harvest. Likewise, children develop protective "skins." A strong-willed child's defiance may actually be a defense against feeling unseen. A quiet or withdrawn child may be guarding a tender heart that fears rejection. Even laughter or busyness can sometimes be coverings for pain. The wise parent learns to ask not only *"What is this behavior?"* but *"What is this behavior protecting?"* That question turns frustration into discernment.

Jesus modeled this perfectly. When the disciples tried to shoo away the noisy children, He was indignant. *"Let the little children come to Me, and do not hinder them, for the kingdom of heaven belongs to such as these"* (Matthew 19:14, NIV). He saw beyond the disruption and recognized divine purpose. In His presence, children were not a distraction from ministry; they were the ministry. He picked them up, blessed them, and showed His followers that true greatness is measured not by stature but by sincerity. When we mirror that attitude, we begin to peel away the fear and hardness that often hide a child's sweetness.

Reaching the inside of a pineapple takes effort. Its tough skin must be cut with precision to avoid wasting the fruit. Parenting works the same way. Peeling too harshly wounds, and cutting too shallow leaves barriers intact. To draw out a child's inner sweetness, love must be steady, discipline consistent, and patience abundant. Harshness bruises the spirit just as surely as a dull knife ruins fruit. *"Fathers, do not provoke your children to anger, but bring them up in the discipline and instruction of the Lord"* (Ephesians 6:4, ESV). Correction that humiliates closes hearts, but correction that teaches opens them. Discipline is not about control; it is about cultivation. The parents' goal is not to break the will but to shape it toward wisdom and self-control.

Inside every child lies sweetness, creativity, empathy, laughter, and faith. That inner treasure refreshes the world. Their prayers invite heaven's attention, and their smiles brighten weary hearts. *"A little child will lead them"* (Isaiah 11:6, NIV). Children's innocence has power; their purity is prophetic. They remind adults what it means to believe without cynicism and to love without condition—parents who slow down to notice this sweetness find that God uses their children to re-teach them joy.

Yet sweetness must be protected by strength. The rind is not an enemy; it is a safeguard. Without structure, the pineapple's golden flesh would rot before it ripens. Likewise, children without boundaries spoil before maturity. *"The rod of correction imparts wisdom, but a child left undisciplined disgraces its mother"* (Proverbs 29:15, NIV). Loving discipline, like the rind, keeps what is good intact until the right season. When parents remove every difficulty or indulge every desire, they risk raising fruit that cannot endure the heat of life. Strength is learned through gentle struggle. Allowing children to experience manageable disappointments builds resilience that preserves sweetness for the long term.

In God's design, strength and tenderness coexist. Jesus Himself embodied this divine balance. He overturned tables in the temple with righteous anger and yet knelt to wash His disciples' feet. He faced the cross with unflinching courage and yet wept at the tomb of Lazarus. His life teaches that gentleness is not weakness, and strength is not cruelty. To raise children in His image means nurturing both traits, teaching them to be firm in conviction yet kind in action, disciplined yet compassionate.

Parents often lean to one side or the other. Some emphasize toughness, wanting their children to be strong, responsible, and fearless. Others emphasize tenderness, focusing on emotions and kindness. But when strength is overdeveloped without compassion, children grow hard. When tenderness is cultivated without discipline, it grows fragile. The beauty of the pineapple is that it keeps both armor and sweetness perfectly balanced. Parents must do the same, building resilience while preserving tenderness.

Practically, this means modeling balance in everyday life. When a parent apologizes after speaking harshly, they show that strength can bow to humility. When they follow through on boundaries even when it is inconvenient, they demonstrate that love can be firm. When they allow children to help with chores, to handle small responsibilities, and to make age-appropriate decisions, they communicate trust. Each of these moments is another careful slice through the rind, revealing more of the sweetness within.

Children raised in this environment learn that emotions are safe but not sovereign, that failure is part of growth, and that love can correct without rejection. They become both strong and gentle, a reflection of Christ Himself. *"By wisdom a house is built, and through understanding it is established; through knowledge its rooms are filled with rare and beautiful treasures"* (Proverbs 24:3–4, NIV). A wise parent builds a home where strength and sweetness dwell together.

The pineapple also symbolizes endurance. It endures months of harsh weather before it ripens, standing upright with its crown intact. Children likewise face pressures from culture, peers, and performance. They need parents who remind them that identity is not found in perfection but in perseverance. *"He who began a good work in you will carry it on to completion"* (Philippians 1:6, NIV). The same God who planted sweetness inside will finish the process of maturity in time. Parents need not panic over temporary thorns; they are part of the growing process.

FRUIT OF THE WOMB

When the fruit is finally opened, its fragrance fills the air. Likewise, when a child's heart is opened through love and wisdom, their sweetness blesses more than just their parents. It spills over into friendships, classrooms, and communities. Their compassion becomes contagious, their faith inspiring. The world hungers for such fruit, lives that are strong enough to stand yet sweet enough to heal.

In many cultures, the pineapple is also a symbol of hospitality, of welcome, warmth, and generosity. When parents nurture the balance of toughness and tenderness in their children, they are raising world changers who refresh others wherever they go. Their kindness becomes an open door, and their resilience becomes a refuge. Such children grow into adults who carry light in dark places because they were taught that gentleness and strength are not opposites but allies.

The pineapple teaches one final lesson. You must be willing to invest time to taste its sweetness. You cannot rush it, and you cannot consume it without preparation. The same is true of parenting. The sweetest results come to those who stay faithful through the seasons, planting in prayer, watering with consistency, and harvesting with gratitude. The fruit of a balanced child is not produced overnight; it is the product of steady love and divine grace.

The message of the pineapple, therefore, is simple yet profound. Strength and sweetness were never meant to compete; they were created to complement. Every child carries both within, and every parent is called to nurture both. God did not design His children to be hard like stone or soft like syrup, but to embody Christ's likeness, courageous and compassionate, bold yet humble, armored yet tender. When parents peel with patience and love, they find that the same child who once resisted instruction becomes the very source of joy and refreshment in the home. Their laughter fills rooms, their prayers move mountains, and their presence testifies to the faithfulness of God. The rough rind becomes evidence of protection, and the sweetness within becomes proof of divine purpose.

Cultivating the Crown: Identity and Resilience

The crown of the pineapple immediately catches the eye, green, upright, and regal. It sits proudly atop the fruit, symbolizing distinction and dignity. Every pineapple wears its crown not as decoration but as identity. It says to the world, *"I am complete."* Likewise, children carry a spiritual crown placed on them by God, a mark of worth, calling, and belonging that no one else can give or take away. Parents have the sacred task of helping their children discover and wear this crown with confidence and humility.

FRUIT OF THE WOMB

Children are not blank slates waiting to be written upon by the world; they are divine creations bearing God's imprint. *"I praise you because I am fearfully and wonderfully made; your works are wonderful"* (Psalm 139:14, NIV). Before they speak their first word or take their first step, heaven has already spoken their identity. Parents who understand this truth will raise their children differently. They will discipline not to control but to confirm identity, correct not to shame but to shape, guide not from fear but from faith in what God has already placed within.

Identity that is rooted in Christ produces resilience. *"We are God's masterpiece, created in Christ Jesus to do good works"* (Ephesians 2:10, NLT). Children who know they are masterpieces do not crumble at criticism nor inflate with praise; they stabilize. This inner crown persuades them to choose conviction over comparison. They stand taller in truth because they know whose image they bear.

Cultivating resilience in children parallels the growth of the pineapple itself. It does not sprout overnight. It takes eighteen to twenty-four months to mature, enduring sun, rain, and wind before bearing fruit. Each stage strengthens the plant to hold its future sweetness. Likewise, children develop resilience through seasons of challenge. *"Consider it pure joy… whenever you face trials… because… the testing of your faith produces perseverance"* (James 1:2–3, NIV). Parents who remove every obstacle rob their children of the opportunity to grow strong. Trials, handled with grace and support, become training grounds for perseverance.

When difficulty comes, a failed test, a strained friendship, a disappointment, rescuing immediately may feel loving, but wisdom asks: what strength might God be building right now? Guidance does not mean control. It means presence, prayer, and perspective. The heat that toughens the pineapple's rind also sweetens its core. So, it is with a child's soul. The same winds that test their faith refine their character.

Families that cultivate resilience become living greenhouses for growth. Parents model perseverance by remaining steadfast in love, consistent in discipline, and calm in storms. They teach children to pray before they panic, to give thanks before they complain, and to seek Scripture before they scroll.

These habits become the inner scaffolding of adulthood, the spiritual muscle that keeps sweetness from collapsing under pressure.

Passing the Fruit: Hospitality, Service, and Legacy

The pineapple has long symbolized hospitality, warmth, generosity, and welcome. In earlier centuries, hosts placed pineapples on banquet tables to announce joy and abundance. Children, likewise, are gifts of divine hospitality: *"Children are a heritage from the*

FRUIT OF THE WOMB

Lord; the fruit of the womb is a reward" (Psalm 127:3, KJV). God entrusts children not merely to brighten a home, but to bless a world. The sweetness you cultivate in them is meant to refresh others.

Hospitality begins at home. Children learn generosity by watching it. When families open their doors, share meals, pray with neighbors, and serve together, children see love in motion. They discover that their crown is for influence, not pride; for blessing, not boasting. Their laughter becomes an invitation; their kindness, a sanctuary. *"Each of you should use whatever gift you have received to serve others"* (1 Peter 4:10, NIV). Service anchored in identity keeps sweetness from turning into self-promotion.

The pineapple also teaches legacy. Though each plant bears one main fruit, its crown and shoots reproduce new plants. One well-cultivated fruit becomes the parent of many. So it is with families. *"Their children will be mighty in the land; the generation of the upright will be blessed"* (Psalm 112:2, NIV). Legacy is not what we leave for our children; it is what we leave in them, faith that endures, character that withstands, love that keeps multiplying when we are gone.

This generational mindset shifts parenting from performance to purpose. We are not raising perfect children; we are shaping enduring legacies. The sweetest harvests are often slow. *"Let us not become weary in doing good, for at the proper time we will reap a harvest if we do not give up"* (Galatians 6:9, NIV). Your prayers today may water a future you will never see; your daily faithfulness may become the crown your grandchildren wear.

When strength and sweetness grow together under the crown of identity, the result is wholeness, believers who can stand firm in adversity yet pour love into others freely. That is the true harvest of godly parenting: children who refresh the world with compassion and endure its pressures with courage; sons and daughters who carry hospitality to strangers and holiness to generations.

FRUIT OF THE WOMB

Reflection Questions

1. Where do I need to better balance strength (boundaries, perseverance) and sweetness (tenderness, encouragement) in my parenting?

2. What words can I speak regularly to affirm my child's God-given identity and "crown"?

3. How can I help my child interpret challenges as training for resilience rather than reasons to quit?

4. In what simple, regular ways can our family practice hospitality so our children learn to bless others?

5. What seeds of faith and character am I intentionally planting now for future generations?

FRUIT OF THE WOMB

A Prayer of Blessing

Lord, you are the wise Gardener who plants purpose in every child. Thank You for the gift of my children, their strength, and their sweetness. Crown them with identity in Christ, guard their tenderness with holy boundaries, and build resilience in every season. Teach me to peel with patience, to correct with compassion, and to model the balance of grace and truth. May their lives refresh others like ripe fruit in a dry land, and may their legacy outlive us to Your glory. In Jesus' name, Amen.

Practical Family Activity – "Pineapple Crown Night"

1. Cut a pineapple together. Invite your child to help peel away the tough rind while you talk about how God protects what is precious within.

2. Share slices and have each person name one way they are strong and one way they are kind.

3. Plant the pineapple crown in soil as a reminder that identity reproduces; pray that God will grow new "fruit" through your family.

FRUIT OF THE WOMB

4. As a family, choose a simple hospitality act for the week (a shared meal, a note of encouragement, or practical help for a neighbor).

5. End with a short blessing spoken over each child by name, affirming their crown, their strength, and their sweetness.

CHAPTER 8

THE ORANGE: WHOLENESS AND HEALING

The orange is one of creation's quiet masterpieces. Its form is simple, yet its symbolism is profound. The moment you hold it in your hand, you feel completeness, the perfect roundness, the fragrant peel, the brightness that speaks of life. Peel it open, and each segment fits neatly beside another, revealing that even the smallest detail of God's creation is designed with harmony and purpose.

In its shape and substance, the orange mirrors the life God intends for every child: balanced, nourished, and whole. Its smooth exterior, juicy core, and radiant color come together to portray what Scripture calls *"shalom"*, peace that is not merely the absence of conflict but the presence of divine order and well-being. The orange tells us that wholeness is not achieved by perfection but by integration. In the same way, children become whole not by excelling in one area but by growing together in body, mind, soul, and spirit under the gentle cultivation of loving parents and a faithful God.

Paul's prayer in 1 Thessalonians 5:23 beautifully captures this desire: *"May God Himself, the God of peace, sanctify you through and through; may your whole spirit, soul, and body be kept blameless at the coming of our Lord Jesus Christ."* The prayer is not limited to adults; it includes the little ones entrusted to our care. God's vision for a child is not partial strength but total harmony: a heart anchored in faith, a mind alive with curiosity, a body filled with vitality, and a spirit open to His voice.

The Wholeness of the Body

The first thing anyone notices about an orange is its vibrancy. Its color draws the eye; its scent awakens the senses. In the same way, a child's physical life is the first window into their wholeness. Scripture calls the body *"a temple of the Holy Spirit"* (1 Corinthians 6:19), reminding us that even the physical dimension of a child's being is sacred. Caring for their health is an act of worship.

Parents sometimes overlook how deeply spiritual physical well-being can be. Sleep, play, nutrition, and movement are not trivial; they are threads in the tapestry of divine design. When children climb, run, dance, or play in the sunlight, they are expressing the joy of their Creator. When families share healthy meals and laughter around the table, they strengthen not only the body but the bonds that keep the heart steady.

The modern world often fractures this balance. Screens replace sunlight, fast food replaces family tables, and constant motion replaces rest. Yet the orange, growing slowly on its tree, teaches patience. It ripens over time, drawing strength from steady roots. Children likewise need rhythms of rest, nourishment, and care to mature in strength and stability. Parents who cultivate these rhythms, family meals, walks together, bedtime blessings, are not simply managing health; they are shaping destiny.

The Wholeness of the Mind

Peel back the skin of an orange, and you'll find a structure that's both orderly and wondrously complex, each segment held together by fine threads, every droplet containing its own sweetness. It's a marvel of design and function. So it is with the human mind, especially the mind of a child. God crafted their intellect with the same intricate beauty, filling it with curiosity and potential.

Children come into the world asking questions long before they understand how vast those questions are. Their wonder is holy; it's a form of worship. Proverbs 25:2 says, *"It is the glory of God to conceal a matter; to search out a matter is the glory of kings."* Every *"why?"* from a child's lips is a small echo of this divine calling to explore. Parents honor God when they nurture curiosity instead of silencing it, when they teach their children not merely what to think but how to think through the lens of truth.

Learning, however, must never be detached from wisdom. Knowledge without character can puff up rather than build up. The orange offers a subtle reminder here: while each section has its own flavor, they all share one source of sweetness. In the same way, a child's intellectual growth must be connected to moral and spiritual roots. Parents who integrate Scripture into learning, who talk about science and God's creation, who see art as an echo of divine creativity, help their children see that all knowledge ultimately points back to its source.

A healthy mind is both informed and inspired. It reasons but also dreams. It remembers facts yet reveres truth. When parents cultivate learning as worship, children discover that study and faith are not rivals but partners in the search for meaning.

The Wholeness of the Soul

At the heart of every orange is a core, a center that holds its segments together. Without that center, the fruit falls apart. This is the image of the soul, the inner life of a child, where emotions, imagination, and relationships dwell. It is here that the deepest needs for love, security, and belonging are formed.

Children are emotionally tender. Their joy is loud, their disappointments piercing, their fears often unspoken. To dismiss their feelings is to dismiss a part of their creation. The Psalms remind us that emotional honesty is sacred; David's prayers were filled with laughter, tears, and everything in between. Parents who listen to their children's hearts teach them that emotions are not enemies to suppress but messages to understand.

Encouragement is the language that waters the soul. Words like *"I'm proud of you," "You matter,"* and *"I love you"* are vitamins for the heart, as vital as any meal. Proverbs 16:24 says, *"Gracious words are a honeycomb, sweet to the soul and healing to the bones."* When spoken consistently, affirming words become the soil in which confidence and compassion grow.

Yet the soul also needs correction, for discipline is a form of love. The orange's peel protects but also defines its shape. Boundaries do the same for the soul of a child; they provide form without crushing freedom. A home filled with affection but void of structure breeds confusion; a home filled with rules but devoid of warmth breeds rebellion. Wholeness flourishes where truth and tenderness walk side by side.

Children who are guided with grace learn that failure is not fatal. They understand that correction does not erase love. Over time, this balance teaches emotional intelligence, the ability to feel deeply yet remain anchored in peace. That is the fruit of a whole soul.

The Wholeness of the Spirit

At its core, the orange carries life, the capacity to refresh, to heal, and to reproduce. This inner vitality mirrors the human spirit, the part of a child that connects most directly with God. It is through the spirit that children hear His whispers, experience wonder, and sense His presence.

Spiritual wholeness begins early. A toddler folding tiny hands in prayer, a school-aged child asking questions about heaven, a teenager sensing conviction, all are signs of a living spirit reaching toward its Maker. Jesus' words in Matthew 19:14 resound with this truth: *"Let the little children come to me, and do not hinder them, for the kingdom of heaven belongs to such as these."* The orange, bright and open once peeled, reminds parents to lead their children toward God, not away from Him, to open their hearts to divine light rather than covering them with doubt.

Parents cultivate the spirit by modeling devotion. Children learn reverence not through lectures but through observation, by seeing their parents pray sincerely, forgive freely, and serve joyfully. Worship at home does not have to be formal; it can be a song sung during chores, gratitude whispered at mealtime, or a bedtime blessing that reminds them, *"God is near."*

When a child's spirit is nurtured, their entire life begins to harmonize. Their mind finds peace, their emotions find grounding, and their body finds rhythm. The Spirit of God becomes the juice that flows through every segment, giving flavor to all they do.

Wholeness as a Parental Calling

The orange challenges every parent to think beyond performance and achievement. The goal is not to raise children who look successful but who live whole. A straight-A student who is anxious and angry is no healthier than an athlete who is admired but spiritually empty. Wholeness is not about doing everything perfectly; it is about aligning each part of life with divine order and love.

Parents who focus only on behavior will peel away the surface without ever tasting the fruit. But those who see beyond outward results and nurture the unseen, faith, joy, curiosity, and empathy will discover the sweetness that lasts. The call is not to manage outcomes but to cultivate integration, to keep body, mind, soul, and Spirit flowing together until the life of the child becomes as complete and radiant as the fruit itself.

The orange, then, becomes a quiet teacher in the home. It says, *Grow steadily. Stay balanced. Protect the tender places. Keep the sweetness within you whole.* When parents heed this lesson, their children not only thrive in their season, they become nourishment to others, carriers of health and harmony in a fractured world.

Healing and Integration

The orange is more than nourishment; it is medicine. Its juice refreshes, its fragrance calms, its vitamin-rich nature restores strength to weary bodies. In its quiet way, it teaches that healing does not always come through grand miracles; it often comes through small, consistent acts of care and renewal. So it is with children. Their laughter can lift a heavy spirit, their hugs can melt anger, and their innocence can heal the cynicism of adulthood.

Every parent has felt it: a child's smile softens frustration, a small voice saying *"I forgive you"* humbles the heart, a bedtime prayer uttered with pure faith reminds us of heaven's closeness. Children carry within them the same healing virtue the orange embodies: restorative, simple, and full of life.

Scripture affirms this healing nature. The prophet Zechariah gave a glimpse of restoration when he said, *"The city streets will be filled with boys and girls playing there"* (Zechariah 8:5, NIV). In other words, when children can laugh freely, society itself has been made whole again. Where children are wounded, silenced, or neglected, communities are sick. But where they play, learn, and flourish, healing flows like fresh juice through dry places.

Healing, however, is not one-sided. Parents, too, are healed through their children. A child's presence has a divine way of confronting the brokenness in adults, the impatience, the unresolved pain, the forgotten tenderness. Children draw out buried emotions and awaken compassion. They remind parents that vulnerability is not weakness but a pathway to grace.

In this way, parenting becomes not only a calling but a mirror. It reveals the unhealed places within us even as it calls us to nurture healing in others. Like the orange, which contains both sweetness and tang, parenting mixes joy and challenge in every slice. The bitterness reminds us we still need grace; the sweetness assures us God's grace is already at work.

Growing Whole Families and Communities

Peel an orange and you'll find a collection of segments, distinct yet joined at the center. That is the picture of a family. Each member has their own personality, calling, and rhythm, but all are bound together by love. When unity and individuality coexist, wholeness thrives.

Families become orchards of healing when they practice connection. A simple meal shared at the table, a gentle apology, a night of laughter, or a bedtime blessing, all these moments are droplets of juice that keep the fruit of family life fresh. Wholeness is not found in perfection but in presence. It is not about erasing differences but weaving them into unity.

Parents must see themselves as cultivators, not controllers. The orange tree does not force each fruit to ripen at the same pace; it gives time and nourishment, trusting the process. Likewise, each child matures differently, some emotionally faster, others intellectually first, and others spiritually deep. When parents honor this diversity, they echo the wisdom of 1 Corinthians 12:12, which teaches that many parts make one body, and each part is essential.

In a spiritually healthy home, discipline and delight coexist. There is room for correction, but there is also room for celebration. There is order, but there is laughter. Just as the peel protects without suffocating, parents must set boundaries that secure the heart yet leave space for the Spirit to breathe. Too much control dries the fruit; too little leaves it unguarded. Love, guided by wisdom, finds the balance.

Wholeness must also extend beyond the household. A family's fruit is meant to feed others. A home that cultivates healing becomes a refuge for neighbors, friends, and even strangers. When visitors enter and sense peace, when children share generously or pray sincerely, the aroma of Christ spreads like the scent of citrus in bloom.

The church, too, must reflect this orchard of wholeness. Too often, children are treated as a side ministry, entertained but not engaged. Yet Jesus said, *"Let the little children come to me, and do not hinder them, for the kingdom of heaven belongs to such as these"* (Matthew 19:14, NIV). When the church welcomes children not as spectators but as worshippers, teachers, and servants-in-training, the body of Christ becomes healthier and more complete.

Imagine a congregation where children lead in prayer, where families serve together, and where intergenerational friendships flourish. That is the kind of orchard God desires, a living community where the sweetness of the Spirit flows freely through every age and season.

Healing Through Adversity

No orange grows without enduring weather. Storms come, winds shake the branches, and yet the fruit ripens in time. Likewise, no family grows without adversity. Wholeness does not mean the absence of hardship; it means learning to draw nourishment from it.

Children face challenges, disappointment, rejection, and loss, but these experiences, guided by loving support, can build resilience rather than ruin. Parents who rush to remove every struggle rob their children of strength. James 1:3 reminds us that *"the testing of your faith produces perseverance."* A child who learns to face setbacks with prayer and encouragement becomes emotionally strong, spiritually grounded, and relationally wise.

Just as an orange's peel thickens under the sun's intensity, adversity strengthens character. What matters is not the absence of heat but the rootedness beneath it. A home that prays together through difficulty produces fruit that endures.

Legacy of Wholeness

Inside every orange are seeds. Each one carries the potential to birth another tree, another generation of fruit. In the same way, every child who grows whole becomes a seed of healing for the next generation. They carry forward not only genetic traits but spiritual patterns.

Psalm 112:2 declares, *"Their children will be mighty in the land; the generation of the upright will be blessed."* When families live with integrity and balance, they plant righteousness that outlives them. Their children become adults who raise others in the same harmony of faith, learning, and love.

Legacy is not measured by possessions left behind but by patterns passed down, patterns of prayer, forgiveness, gratitude, and grace. A child raised in wholeness becomes a parent who repeats it. The fruit multiplies, the orchard expands, and the fragrance of God's peace fills the generations.

Reflection Questions

1. How can I help my child experience healing in the areas where they may be hurt or fragmented?

2. What practices in our home promote wholeness, and which ones might be pulling us apart?

3. Do I allow my child to face challenges in ways that strengthen their faith and resilience?

4. How can our family extend healing beyond our household, into our church, school, or community?

5. What seeds of wholeness am I planting today that will shape my children's future legacy?

A Prayer of Blessing

Father, thank You for being the source of wholeness and healing. I lift my children before You, asking that every part of their lives, body, mind, soul, and Spirit, be brought into harmony under Your care. Heal what is wounded, strengthen what is weak, and renew what is weary. Let our home become an orchard of peace where Your presence dwells, and may the fruit of our love refresh others. Make our family whole, that we might reveal Your wholeness to the world. In Jesus' name, Amen.

Practical Family Activity – "Orange Wholeness Night"

1. Gather as a family around a table with a bowl of fresh oranges.

2. Peel one together, separating the segments. Talk about how each piece is unique, yet all belong to one fruit.

3. Have each person share one part of their life they feel healthy in, and one area where they need God's healing.

4. Eat the orange together, thanking God for balance, growth, and restoration.

5. Close with a prayer of gratitude: *"Lord, make us whole, each part, each heart, each generation."*

CHAPTER 9

THE STRAWBERRY: TENDERNESS AND GROWTH IN LOW PLACES

The strawberry is one of the gentlest fruits in creation. It grows low to the ground, wrapped in tender leaves, its scarlet body glistening with sweetness yet easily bruised by careless touch. It does not climb like the vine or hang high like the mango; it finds its beauty in humility. Its fragrance is delicate, its flesh soft, its sweetness unforced. The strawberry teaches us that strength is not always loud, tall, or unyielding. Sometimes it is soft, small, and humble, and that is enough.

Children are God's living strawberries. They grow in tender places, fragile yet filled with life, easily wounded yet capable of remarkable sweetness. The strength of a child is not measured in physical power or confidence, but in the purity of heart that reflects heaven. Their laughter heals tension, their questions spark wisdom, and their trust disarms fear. Their vulnerability carries a mysterious kind of power, the power to soften what has grown hard and to awaken what has grown numb.

Psalm 8:2 says, *"Through the praise of children and infants you have established a stronghold against your enemies, to silence the foe and the avenger."* The Scripture reminds us that God uses the voices of children, their songs, their innocence, their unguarded praise, as a fortress of strength. In their openness, He reveals His glory. Tenderness, when joined with purity, becomes a force that darkness cannot imitate or defeat.

Parents, then, are called to treat tenderness not as weakness to overcome but as treasure to guard. The culture around us prizes toughness and self-reliance; it rewards children who seem "mature for their age" and dismisses those who feel deeply or cry easily. Yet the very qualities the world undervalues are the ones heaven celebrates. The gentle heart, the kind word, the empathetic spirit, these are the seeds of greatness in God's eyes. When parents rush to make children "strong," they often mistake hardness for strength and independence for growth. True strength is not the absence of emotion but the ability to love without fear.

Jesus modeled this beautifully. Though He could command storms and silence demons, He was never ashamed to weep. Standing at Lazarus' tomb, *"Jesus wept"* (John 11:35). Those two words have comforted generations because they reveal that divine strength includes divine sensitivity. The Son of God was no less powerful because He felt grief; He was more complete. His tears sanctified emotion, proving that tenderness and authority can coexist. Parents who mirror Christ in this way, strong enough to lead yet tender enough to feel, teach their children that wholeness includes both firmness and compassion.

Tenderness is the soil where faith and love grow. A hardened heart cannot absorb truth, just as parched soil resists rain. The strawberry thrives because the earth around it stays soft and moist, welcoming nourishment. In the same way, children flourish in homes where warmth, patience, and kindness prevail. Harshness may control behavior for a moment, but tenderness shapes the heart for a lifetime. It turns discipline into discipleship and correction into cultivation. The words we choose when children falter are like the hands that pick strawberries: too rough, and we crush what we are trying to save.

Proverbs 15:1 tells us, *"A gentle answer turns away wrath, but a harsh word stirs up anger."* The tone of our voice, the expression on our face, the timing of our correction, all these can either bruise or bless. A gentle response can stop rebellion before it begins. A harsh one can wound even when the intention is love. Parents must learn to speak life the way a gardener handles fruit, with steady, patient care.

There is quiet courage in tenderness. The strawberry's softness allows it to absorb light, moisture, and nourishment that harder fruits might repel. In the same way, a tender-hearted child absorbs wisdom and love easily. Their sensitivity makes them teachable, impressionable in the best way. A child whose emotions are acknowledged learns trust; a child who is dismissed learns distance. When a child feels safe to feel, they begin to grow toward God rather than away from Him.

Tenderness also keeps the spirit alert to the presence of God. Many adults lose the ability to feel deeply because life hardens them. Yet children seem to sense God's nearness naturally. Their prayers are simple but sincere; their faith uncomplicated but profound. When Jesus said, *"Let the little children come to me, and do not hinder them, for the kingdom of heaven belongs to such as these"* (Matthew 19:14), He was pointing to the spiritual purity that tenderness makes possible. A heart that stays soft before God is a heart that hears Him clearly.

The world will try to teach children that vulnerability is dangerous, that sensitivity is shameful, and that strength means silence. Parents must resist this distortion by celebrating emotion as part of God's image in us. Children must know that tears are not failure, that feeling deeply is holy, and that kindness is not naivety. When a child learns to connect emotion with faith, empathy with prayer, and compassion with courage, tenderness becomes their greatest strength.

FRUIT OF THE WOMB

In homes shaped by gentleness, children thrive. They learn that correction is not rejection, that forgiveness is stronger than punishment, and that love never withdraws even when discipline is firm. They discover that they can make mistakes without losing belonging. This emotional safety is what gives them confidence to grow. It is the spiritual equivalent of sunlight for the strawberry, constant, warm, and life-giving.

The fruit of such tenderness is visible in later years. Children raised in gentleness often become adults who bring peace into chaotic rooms. They carry an inner calm that disarms hostility. Their sensitivity makes them aware of others' pain, and their compassion compels them to act. They become counselors, intercessors, healers, and creators, people who rebuild what others have broken.

Parents who nurture tenderness are not raising fragile children; they are raising restorers. The same softness that makes strawberries bruise easily also makes them irresistible and nourishing. Likewise, the same sensitivity that makes children cry easily often makes them love deeply. And love, true, unconditional, enduring love, is the rarest and strongest fruit of all.

Tenderness, then, is not something to outgrow but something to grow into. It matures into wisdom, expands into empathy, and ripens into grace. Parents must teach their children to keep their hearts tender even when the world grows hard. It is tenderness that keeps faith alive, relationships healthy, and hope renewed. A child who learns to stay soft in spirit will never lose their sweetness, even in seasons of struggle.

The strawberry teaches this truth silently, season after season. It never competes for height or dominance; it simply offers what it has: beauty, nourishment, and delight. Its life is lived close to the soil, near the source of its strength. So it is with children whose hearts remain tender before God. They may not stand tallest or speak loudest, but their presence fills the world with fragrance and color. They teach us, in their quiet way, that strength is not the ability to resist touch but the courage to remain open to it.

Growing in Low Places

The strawberry does not grow on lofty branches or winding vines that stretch toward the sun. It finds its home close to the soil, humble and hidden beneath its leaves. Its beauty lies in its lowliness, its sweetness in its nearness to the ground. This posture teaches a profound truth: greatness often begins in low places.

Children, too, begin their lives close to the ground, dependent, small, and unseen by the grand systems of the world. They do not come into life demanding recognition; they arrive needing nurture. Their strength develops not in height but in humility. Like strawberries that thrive best when planted low and tended carefully, children flourish when they grow in environments of grace, consistency, and closeness.

The world tends to admire what rises high: ambition, independence, and visibility. But God often begins His greatest works in low and hidden places. Scripture is full of people whose humble beginnings prepared them for holy purposes. David, the future king, was first a shepherd boy in the forgotten fields of Bethlehem. Samuel, the prophet who would anoint kings, first learned to listen to God's voice as a child in the quiet chambers of the temple. Even our Savior, Jesus Christ, began His earthly life in a manager. None of these grew from prestige or position; their fruit ripened in obscurity, watered by humility and faith.

The strawberry's closeness to the earth symbolizes dependence, its roots constantly drawing nourishment from the soil. So too must children remain connected to their roots: their families, their faith, and their identity in God. Parents play the role of soil, the environment that surrounds, nourishes, and anchors their growth—the richer and more stable the soil, the sweeter the fruit. When homes are filled with love, forgiveness, and stability, children grow with peace.

FRUIT OF THE WOMB

When homes are marked by harshness or inconsistency, their development becomes stunted, and their sweetness is delayed.

To grow in low places also means to value hidden growth. Parents often focus on what is visible: grades, achievements, and milestones. But the most important growth happens beneath the surface. It happens in the unseen spaces of the heart where character, integrity, and faith take root. Like the strawberry's roots spreading quietly beneath the soil, a child's spiritual and emotional foundations develop silently but steadily. Patience, honesty, gratitude, and humility cannot be measured in test scores, but they are the true indicators of wholeness.

God calls parents to slow down and tend to the unseen. To water their children's hearts with encouragement. To nourish them with truth. To cover them with prayer. To remove the weeds of fear and comparison that choke growth. Parenting in low places is not glamorous, but it is sacred. It means bending low, listening more than speaking, and finding joy in the ordinary rhythms of nurture.

The low place is also a place of safety. Strawberries growing near the ground are sheltered by their leaves from harsh winds. Likewise, children flourish when covered by love, guidance, and prayer. The parental covering is not about control but about protection, creating a space where innocence can mature into wisdom without being prematurely exposed to harm. Proverbs 4:23 reminds us, *"Above all else, guard your heart, for everything you do flows from it."* The same principle applies to the hearts of children: they must be guarded, not by walls of fear, but by shields of wisdom.

And yet, humility is not just the beginning of growth; it is the secret of continued fruitfulness. Even as children grow older and stronger, parents must remind them that the sweetest fruit remains close to the ground. When young people learn to stay humble amid achievement, to remain kind in success, and to serve even when celebrated, they preserve the tenderness that makes their greatness beautiful.

Sweetness That Multiplies

If the strawberry teaches us anything beyond tenderness and humility, it is generosity. Its sweetness was never meant to be hidden. The strawberry ripens not for itself but for others. It gives its fragrance freely to the air, its color to the garden, and its taste to every table. It embodies the principle of fruitfulness that multiplies.

Children mirror this truth. The sweetness of their hearts, once nurtured, spreads naturally to everyone around them. A kind child softens a classroom. A gentle word from a sibling restores peace in the home. A prayer from a young believer revives faith in a discouraged heart. Their influence multiplies without effort because tenderness, when cultivated, becomes contagious.

FRUIT OF THE WOMB

The strawberry plant is also a marvel of multiplication. From one plant, runners stretch outward, taking root to produce new life. Over time, a single berry patch becomes a bed of fruit. In the same way, children who are raised in love and humility carry that same sweetness into their friendships, families, and future generations. Compassion, once planted, creates communities of care. A child raised to forgive will raise children who forgive. A child who grows in kindness will build workplaces of honor and families of peace.

Proverbs 17:6 says, *"Children's children are a crown to the aged, and parents are the pride of their children."* The strawberry reminds us that parenting is not only about producing fruit in the present but also about sowing sweetness into the future. The tenderness parents nurture today becomes a legacy tomorrow. The words spoken in patience, the hugs given after tears, the prayers whispered in faith, all these are runners stretching into the next generation, taking root in hearts we may never see.

Even fragility has its role in multiplication. Strawberries bruise easily, yet their seeds are carried even when the fruit is crushed. Likewise, children may be hurt by life's trials, but when grounded in God's love, their brokenness often becomes the very place where new compassion grows. The Apostle Paul reminds us in 2 Corinthians 12:9, *"My grace is sufficient for you, for my power is made perfect in weakness."* A tender heart that has been healed becomes twice as powerful, strong enough to feel, yet wise enough to help others heal, too.

The strawberry's sweetness also symbolizes purpose. It exists not for survival but for delight. Likewise, children are not given simply to fill homes with laughter or to continue a family name. They are divine gifts meant to reveal God's joy to the world. When parents raise children with this vision, to live not for themselves but to bless others, their families become gardens of grace.

True fruitfulness is never about quantity alone but about quality, the kind of love, humility, and character that leaves a lasting impression. A single act of kindness from a child can outlive generations of achievements. A forgiving spirit can mend what authority alone could not. Like strawberries gathered and shared at the table, the sweetness of a godly child feeds more than one life.

As children mature, parents must help them see that their sweetness is not a possession to hoard but a calling to steward. The tenderness that once needed protection must become compassion in action. They are to serve, to give, to love, and to shine. The fruit of the womb is not meant to stay hidden under leaves but to brighten the world with God's goodness.

When parents live this truth, they become the first partakers of the fruit they have cultivated. Their children's joy becomes their joy.

FRUIT OF THE WOMB

Their children's faith becomes their testimony. Their children's sweetness becomes their crown.

FRUIT OF THE WOMB

Reflection Questions

1. How do I respond to my child's tenderness, with understanding or with impatience?

2. In what ways can I create a "low place" in my home where humility and connection thrive?

3. Do I value hidden growth as much as visible achievement in my child's life?

4. How am I nurturing qualities in my children that will multiply and bless future generations?

5. What habits of love, forgiveness, or compassion can I sow today that will bear fruit tomorrow?

FRUIT OF THE WOMB

A Prayer of Blessing

Heavenly Father,

Thank You for the tender beauty of children, for hearts that love easily, forgive quickly, and reflect Your gentleness. Teach me to handle their souls with care, to guard their innocence without fear, and to celebrate their softness as strength. Help me to bend low like the strawberry, humble and near to the ground, drawing life from Your presence. May my children grow in humility, rooted in faith, spreading sweetness wherever they go. Let their tenderness become healing for others and their humility a testimony of Your grace. In Jesus' name, Amen.

Practical Family Activity – "Strawberry Blessing Night"

1. Gather a bowl of strawberries and place them at the center of the family table.

2. Before eating, hold one strawberry and say: *"This fruit grows close to the ground, just like God calls us to stay humble and tender."*

3. Invite each family member to share one tender or kind quality they see in another.

FRUIT OF THE WOMB

4. Parents affirm each child by naming a way their tenderness blesses the family or community.

5. As you enjoy the strawberries together, pray aloud, thanking God for making your home a garden of sweetness and humility that multiplies for generations.

CHAPTER 10

THE COCONUT: LAYERS OF DISCOVERY

Few fruits capture the mystery of divine design like the coconut. From the outside, it seems unremarkable, rough, fibrous, and difficult to open. Yet those who take the time to look closer discover layer after layer of purpose. Beneath the coarse husk lies a hard shell. Beneath that shell, sweet water and nourishing meat. Each layer contributes to the fruit's wholeness and survival. Nothing is wasted. Every detail speaks of intentional creation.

Children, too, are beautifully layered. They are not simple beings who can be understood at a glance. Each child is a composition of body, mind, soul, and spirit, a living masterpiece that God Himself shaped with precision. Psalm 139:14 declares, "I praise You because I am fearfully and wonderfully made; Your works are wonderful, I know that full well." Within every child lies depth waiting to be discovered, beauty waiting to be revealed, and potential waiting to be nurtured.

The outer husk of a coconut is like the visible behavior of a child. It is what others see first, moods, mannerisms, energy levels, expressions, or even shyness. Parents often form judgments based on this surface layer, assuming that what they see is the whole picture. A wise parent understands that behavior is only the husk, not the heart. Beneath it lies the unseen story, a mix of emotions, dreams, fears, and gifts that shape who the child truly is.

Some children appear quiet and reserved, yet within them burns the spark of creativity and compassion. Others are lively and outspoken, carrying the seeds of leadership and courage. Still others are sensitive, thoughtful, or deeply spiritual. The husk protects these qualities until the right time. When parents look beyond the outer behavior, they begin to see the divine craftsmanship hidden within. The key is patience. Just as no one discovers the sweetness of coconut water without effort, no parent can discover a child's inner treasure without time, observation, and love.

God has entrusted parents with the sacred task of peeling back these layers, not through pressure or force, but through relationship. Conversations at bedtime, shared laughter, listening without interruption, these are the gentle tools that unlock a child's inner world. Proverbs 20:5 reminds us, "The purposes of a person's heart are deep waters, but one who has insight draws them out." Every child is a well of deep water. Parents must become skillful at drawing it forth.

When the coconut is unopened, its value is hidden. In the same way, a child's greatness is often unseen until someone takes the time to draw it out. The process may not be easy, but every layer is sacred. The more we peel, the more we understand that God's design for children is not surface-deep. It is layered with wonder.

The Beauty Beneath the Hard Shell

Beneath the husk of the coconut lies its thick, solid shell, tough, unyielding, and essential. Without this shell, the delicate water and tender meat inside would never survive the elements.

The shell protects the life within. Likewise, children need boundaries, discipline, and guidance that form the moral and emotional "shell" around their inner life.

Discipline is not punishment. It is protection. It is the boundary that keeps innocence from being stolen and character from being spoiled. Proverbs 29:15 tells us, "The rod of correction imparts wisdom, but a child left undisciplined disgraces its mother." The rod here is not an instrument of fear, but of direction. A loving parent disciplines not to harm, but to preserve. Just as the shell of a coconut guards its contents, healthy discipline shields a child's heart from confusion and destruction.

Children thrive within structure. They may resist boundaries in the moment, but deep down, they crave the stability those boundaries bring. A child without guidance feels exposed, uncertain, and unsafe. The shell gives form to freedom. It provides the safety within which the child can explore, learn, and grow.

In a world that often mistakes freedom for the absence of rules, parents must remember that boundaries are gifts. They teach responsibility, accountability, and respect. A child who learns to honor limits at home will carry that wisdom into every area of life. When discipline is rooted in love rather than anger, it builds trust instead of fear.

Parents must also discern balance. Too hard a shell can suffocate the growth within. Too soft a shell leaves the inner layers vulnerable. Godly discipline mirrors the gentleness and firmness of His own nature, merciful yet just, compassionate yet steadfast. The goal is not control, but character. Not compliance, but connection.

When parents lovingly correct, they echo the heart of God, who shapes His children not through condemnation, but through care. Hebrews 12:6 declares, "The Lord disciplines those He loves." The firmness of God's hand is always guided by affection. Likewise, the firmness of a parent's voice should always be guided by love.

The beauty of the coconut lies in what the shell protects, the sweetness and life within. So it is with children. Beneath the discipline, there is joy. Beneath the structure, there is safety. Beneath the correction, there is growth. Parents who hold their children firmly yet tenderly will one day see the fruit of their patience ripen into maturity.

When the shell of a coconut is finally cracked, a sweet reward is revealed, clear, refreshing water. This is the living spirit of the fruit, the part that refreshes and renews. In the same way, the spirit of a child is God-breathed and alive. It carries innocence, joy, and a natural sensitivity to the presence of God. Jesus said in Matthew 19:14, "Let the little children come to me, and do not hinder them, for the kingdom of heaven belongs to such as these."

Children's spirits often sense God's nearness long before they can articulate it. They believe easily, worship freely, and love without pretense. Their spiritual vitality is pure like coconut water, untouched and refreshing to all who encounter it. Parents who nurture this layer of their children's being teach them that God is not distant, but deeply personal. Prayer becomes as natural as breathing, and worship flows from a heart that has not yet been hardened by cynicism or fear.

This inner water must be protected. A child's spirit can be wounded by ridicule, neglect, or disbelief. When their expressions of faith are mocked or ignored, they may retreat inward, unsure if God listens to little voices. Wise parents create space for their children's faith to grow by praying together, reading Scripture aloud, and affirming the ways they see God at work in their child's life. These small moments pour living water into their spirits and strengthen their connection to God.

Beneath that water lies another layer, the white, nourishing meat of the coconut. This layer represents the mind and soul of a child, the seat of thought, emotion, and identity. Just as the coconut meat sustains life, this layer sustains personality and purpose. A nourished soul produces confidence, empathy, and wisdom. A nourished mind produces creativity, curiosity, and intelligence. Together, they form the child's sense of wholeness.

Parents are the primary cultivators of this nourishment. Feeding the mind involves exposure to knowledge, storytelling, discovery, and play. Feeding the soul involves love, affirmation, forgiveness, and belonging. When these are neglected, children may become intellectually bright but emotionally hungry, or spiritually aware but mentally untrained. Both must grow together.

Deuteronomy 6:6–7 gives practical wisdom for this balance, "These commandments that I give you today are to be on your hearts. Impress them on your children. Talk about them when you sit at home and when you walk along the road, when you lie down and when you get up." This verse reminds us that teaching is not confined to classrooms. It happens in everyday life. Family conversations, shared meals, bedtime prayers, and even moments of correction are all opportunities to feed a child's mind and soul.

As parents peel away layers of misunderstanding or insecurity in their children, they uncover gifts and insights hidden deep within. Like the sweetness locked inside the coconut, the best of a child often requires effort to discover. The process demands time, attentiveness, and patience. No one learns a child by rushing them. It is only through consistent love, listening, and prayerful discernment that the heart's treasure is revealed.

Wholeness Through Every Layer

A coconut's strength lies in its integration, each part working in harmony. The husk, shell, water, and meat all serve a purpose, and together they preserve the fruit's wholeness. Remove one, and the fruit begins to decay. The same is true of children. They are not made of separate compartments, but of connected layers, body, mind, soul, and spirit, that thrive together.

Parents must therefore resist the temptation to overdevelop one layer while neglecting others. Some focus solely on academic excellence, while others emphasize physical or spiritual growth at the expense of emotional health. God's design for wholeness is holistic. He calls parents to nurture every layer, ensuring balance and integration.

FRUIT OF THE WOMB

The Apostle Paul prayed in 1 Thessalonians 5:23, "May God Himself, the God of peace, sanctify you through and through. May your whole spirit, soul, and body be kept blameless at the coming of our Lord Jesus Christ." That prayer extends to children. They are not meant to grow spiritually while collapsing emotionally, nor to excel intellectually while starving spiritually. God desires complete harmony.

Resilience grows from this integration. The coconut survives harsh winds and falls from great heights because its layers work together. In the same way, a child who is spiritually anchored, emotionally affirmed, mentally challenged, and physically cared for can withstand life's pressures. They may stumble, but they will not shatter.

Resilience does not mean invulnerability. It means the ability to recover. When a coconut hits the ground, it does not lose its water. The same is true of children filled with God's presence. Their peace, like the water within, endures through difficulty. Isaiah 54:13 declares, "All your children will be taught by the Lord, and great will be their peace." That peace is the product of balanced, layered nurturing.

Wholeness also speaks of legacy. Every coconut holds within it the seed for another tree. When it falls, takes root, and grows, it multiplies its kind. Similarly, when children are raised in wholeness, they become carriers of blessing for generations. Psalm 78: 4–6 urges, "We will tell the next generation the praiseworthy deeds of the Lord, so the next generation would know them, even the children yet to be born." Parents who invest in each layer of their child's being are not merely shaping one life. They are influencing future families, communities, and nations.

The coconut gives everything it contains. Its water refreshes, its meat nourishes, its shell protects, and its husk becomes fuel. Children, too, are created to give. When raised in love and balance, they become healers, leaders, thinkers, and servants. Their gifts flow outward to bless the world. Jesus said in Matthew 5:14, "You are the light of the world." Parents who nurture every layer equip their children to shine that light brightly.

Finally, the coconut reminds us that discovery is lifelong. Parents never fully exhaust the mystery of who their children are. Each season reveals new layers, childhood curiosity, teenage independence, and adult purpose. Parenting is a continual unveiling of God's design, calling for humility and wonder. Just as every coconut contains more than meets the eye, every child carries depths that even the most loving parents are still discovering.

Reflection Questions

Am I nurturing every layer of my child's body, mind, soul, and spirit, or focusing too heavily on one area?

How can I become more patient in discovering the treasures hidden within my child's heart?

In what ways do I model balance and wholeness for my children?

How can I help my child see their life as a gift meant to bless others?

What legacy of faith, resilience, and wholeness am I planting in my child today?

FRUIT OF THE WOMB

A Prayer of Blessing

Heavenly Father, thank You for creating children as layered and wonderful as the coconut, strong on the outside, yet filled with sweetness and life within. Teach me to nurture every layer of their being with love, patience, and wisdom. Help me to see beyond the surface, to reach their heart, and to draw out the treasures You placed inside them. Strengthen their spirit, nourish their mind, and anchor their soul in Your Word. May they grow resilient, whole, and fruitful, carrying refreshment and healing to everyone they meet. In Jesus' name, Amen.

Practical Family Activity – "Coconut Layers Night"

1. **Gather a coconut** as a family. Examine its husk and shell, talking about how tough it looks on the outside.
2. **Work together** to open it. Pour the water into cups and share it, saying, "This water is like the spirit God placed inside us, pure and refreshing."
3. **Taste the coconut meat** and discuss how each part, the husk, shell, water, and meat, serves a purpose.
4. **Reflect aloud**, "God made each of us with layers, our body, mind, soul, and spirit. When all parts are cared for, we become whole."

5. **Close in prayer**, thanking God for making the family strong, layered, and full of life.

CHAPTER 11

THE LEMON: RESILIENCE THROUGH SOUR SEASONS

The lemon is among nature's most remarkable paradoxes. It dazzles the eye with brightness yet startles the tongue with sourness. Its outer skin shines with beauty, but its flavor shocks with intensity. No one bites into a lemon expecting sweetness, yet few fruits are as essential. The lemon heals, cleanses, refreshes, and preserves. It cuts through dullness and revives taste. It reminds us that what seems unpleasant at first can be profoundly purposeful in the hands of the Creator.

Children's lives often reflect this same divine paradox. There are delightful seasons of sweetness and lighthearted joy, but also sour seasons. These are the moments when attitudes clash, wills collide, and growth stretches both the child and the parent. A toddler may assert independence with tantrums. A school-aged child may resist instruction. A teenager may question faith or challenge authority. In these moments, parenting can feel like tasting pure lemon, sharp, shocking, and uncomfortable. Yet beneath that sting lies something transformative. The sour seasons are the soul's cleansing agents.

FRUIT OF THE WOMB

They purify, strengthen, and prepare both children and parents for maturity.

The Apostle James wrote, "Consider it pure joy, my brothers and sisters, whenever you face trials of many kinds, because you know that the testing of your faith produces perseverance" (James 1:2–3, NIV). Trials, though unwelcome, build endurance. The same principle applies to raising children. The difficult phases of growth are not punishments. They are processes. They test love, expose weaknesses, and ultimately produce wisdom. A lemon's sourness awakens the senses. Likewise, a child's resistance can awaken deeper patience, creativity, and prayer in a parent's heart.

It is tempting to crave only sweetness from our children, compliance, gratitude, and calm, but sweetness without sharpness leads to shallowness. A life without tension never deepens. Just as lemon juice prevents spoilage in food, seasons of correction prevent moral and emotional decay. When guided with grace, even confrontation becomes cleansing. The sharp words exchanged in correction, the tears that accompany repentance, and the boundaries set in love all serve as spiritual vitamin C for the soul. They strengthen what immaturity would otherwise weaken.

Parents who endure the sour seasons faithfully often emerge transformed. The moments that once felt like failures become memories of growth. What once seemed bitter becomes, in hindsight, the essential acidity that gave life its depth. The lemon teaches us that God can use the sour to refine, the sting to purify, and the shock to awaken dormant grace.

God Himself models this balance. He disciplines His children not to destroy but to develop. Hebrews 12:10–11 (AMP) declares, "He disciplines us for our good, so that we may share His holiness. For the moment, all discipline seems painful rather than pleasant, but later it yields the peaceful fruit of righteousness." Divine discipline, like lemon juice on a wound, stings only to heal. It removes infection and restores purity. Parents who mirror this divine pattern raise children who understand that correction is not rejection, but love in motion.

The lemon's bright yellow skin also tells another story, hope. Its color symbolizes joy and vitality. Though its flavor is sharp, its appearance is radiant. God often hides joy inside struggle, just as He hides nourishment inside sourness. Parents who learn to look for light even in testing seasons discover that every challenge conceals a reason for gratitude. Growth is never wasted.

When a child resists instruction, it may be the early stirring of independence that one day becomes leadership. When a teen questions faith, it may be the search for authentic belief that matures into conviction. The parents' task is not to crush the sharpness but to channel it. Just as a cook learns to harness lemon's power to enhance flavor, wise parents learn to use tension to enhance growth.

In every household, the lemon sits on the counter as a reminder. Life's sharp moments are ingredients of purpose. They are not signs of failure, but of fermentation, something being refined beneath the surface. God often sweetens what was once sour through the gentle process of time, patience, and prayer.

The Cleansing Work of Sour Seasons

Perhaps the lemon's most profound gift is its ability to cleanse. It detoxifies what is impure, brightens what is dull, and brings freshness where stagnation once lingered. Similarly, the sour seasons in a child's life serve a cleansing purpose. They expose what lies beneath the surface, attitudes, fears, or weaknesses, and offer an opportunity for renewal.

A child who faces failure learns humility. A teenager who experiences rejection learns empathy. A family that endures conflict learns forgiveness. These lessons cannot be taught through comfort alone. They require friction, challenge, and the sting of correction. Sourness, when submitted to God, becomes sanctifying.

FRUIT OF THE WOMB

Proverbs 3: 11–12 (NLT) says, "My child, don't reject the Lord's discipline, and don't be upset when he corrects you. For the Lord corrects those he loves, just as a father corrects a child in whom he delights." This passage reveals that divine correction is rooted in delight, not disappointment. God cleanses because He loves. Likewise, parents who lovingly guide their children through sour seasons are cooperating with heaven's refining process.

Think of lemon juice applied to a cut. It burns, but it cleans. It disinfects what could otherwise fester. The same is true when parents confront wrong behavior. The sting of consequence purifies the heart. A gentle but firm boundary, a fair discipline, or a necessary "no" are all instruments of cleansing. They teach self-control and accountability, virtues essential to resilience.

Parents who refuse to address sour behavior often mistake leniency for love. Yet avoidance allows decay to spread unseen. The absence of correction may feel peaceful for the moment, but it produces deeper pain later. Like a fruit left unwashed, an uncorrected heart eventually spoils. Wise parents recognize that a season of discomfort is far better than a lifetime of disorder.

Sour seasons also cleanse parents. When a child rebels or struggles, it reveals areas in the parent's heart that need patience, forgiveness, or faith. The process is humbling. It draws parents to prayer, forces them to rely on grace, and teaches dependence on God's wisdom rather than human control. Parenting is never one-sided. As children grow, so do parents. Both are being refined together.

The Bible offers powerful examples of this cleansing principle. Joseph endured betrayal and imprisonment before ruling Egypt. Those bitter years removed arrogance and birthed humility. David fled from Saul before ascending the throne. The caves of adversity cleansed him of self-reliance. Even Jesus "learned obedience from what He suffered" (Hebrews 5:8). God's most fruitful servants often emerge from seasons of sour refinement.

In family life, this means that tension has purpose. The conflicts of adolescence, the tears of misunderstanding, the weariness of correction, all of these are stages of cleansing. The Holy Spirit uses them to wash away selfishness, pride, or fear from both child and parent. When viewed through faith's lens, even the most frustrating moments become opportunities for sanctification.

The lemon also cleanses the air with its fragrance. In the same way, a home that yields to God's refining work begins to carry a spiritual freshness. Bitterness is replaced by gratitude. Complaint gives way to contentment. The family atmosphere changes, not because circumstances are perfect, but because hearts have been purified.

The sourness that once felt unbearable becomes the fragrance of renewal.

It is not easy to embrace this process. No one enjoys the sting of lemon on tender skin or the bite of correction on a tender heart. Yet parents who persist in love discover the hidden sweetness that follows. The same lemon that burns also brightens. The same trial that hurts also heals. What God allows to sting is the very thing He uses to strengthen.

Over time, parents who choose prayer over panic begin to see the fruit of their endurance. Their children emerge wiser, humbler, and more grounded. The home becomes a place where sourness no longer signals defeat but development. It becomes understood that pain can purify, boundaries can bless, and struggle can sanctify. The family learns together that grace is not always sugar. It is sometimes lemon, too.

From Sourness to Strength

If sourness represents struggle, then strength is its refined sweetness. The transformation of a lemon into lemonade is more than a kitchen act. It is a metaphor for redemption. The sourness never disappears; it is simply mixed with new ingredients that draw out its hidden beauty. The sting becomes refreshment. The bitterness becomes balanced. Likewise, the difficulties children and parents face are not wasted. God mixes them with grace, wisdom, and love to produce resilience, the mature strength that endures long after the sour season ends.

Resilience is not born in comfort. It is forged in adversity, in the daily challenges of learning obedience, coping with disappointment, or navigating misunderstanding. When a child struggles to control emotions, fails at a task, or faces rejection, something unseen is forming: endurance. Each sour experience trains the will to persevere and the heart to hope. Like the lemon's acidity that strengthens the immune system, life's challenges fortify a child's inner world.

Romans 5:3–4 (NLT) teaches, "We can rejoice, too, when we run into problems and trials, for we know that they help us develop endurance. And endurance develops strength of character, and character strengthens our confident hope of salvation." Every challenge a child faces, and every moment a parent chooses patience over panic, is part of God's refining process. The sour seasons that seem to unsettle the home are often the very moments God uses to build spiritual muscle.

Resilience does not mean hardening the heart. A lemon's outer skin is firm, but inside it remains juicy and alive. True strength allows feeling but refuses defeat. Parents must teach their children that being strong does not mean being unfeeling. The ability to cry, apologize, or try again after failure is the essence of spiritual maturity. The Apostle Paul declared, "When I am weak, then I am strong" (2 Corinthians 12:10). Strength in the kingdom of God is not the absence of emotion; it is the presence of perseverance.

Parents also grow through this process. Each sour phase becomes a classroom for humility. When a child challenges authority or tests limits, the parent must choose between reaction and reflection. Will I lash out, or will I lean on God? Will I demand control, or will I model grace? Over time, these decisions transform parenting from mere management into ministry. Parents who remain faithful through their children's sour phases become living portraits of God's patience toward His own children.

God's parenting style is instructive here. He does not remove sourness; He redeems it. The Israelites wandered forty years through wilderness discipline, yet through those trials, God forged identity and resilience. The early disciples faced persecution and misunderstanding, yet from that hardship the Church grew strong. Parents can take comfort in this divine pattern. Nothing sour is wasted when placed in God's hands.

When sour seasons come, perspective is key. Parents who see only behavior may react with frustration, but those who know the heart will respond with wisdom. A sour attitude might be hiding fear. Rebellion might be masking insecurity. Children, like lemons, have layers, skin that protects tenderness within. Instead of crushing the fruit to reach the sweetness, wise parents patiently peel, listen, and guide. It is through that gentleness that true transformation happens.

Over time, the sourness that once strained the relationship becomes the very story that strengthens it. Parents and children look back and see how endurance shaped empathy, how correction birthed confidence, and how challenge deepened faith. Sour seasons do not last forever, but the strength they produce does.

Even Jesus experienced this transformation. The vinegar He tasted on the cross was the final note of His suffering, the sourness of sin absorbed and transformed by divine love. Out of that bitterness came the sweetness of salvation. The cross stands as the ultimate picture of how God turns sour into strength, pain into purpose, and suffering into redemption.

Parents who walk through hard seasons with their children participate in that same redemptive rhythm. They bear the sourness of misunderstanding, discipline, or exhaustion, not in vain, but as partners with Christ in forming resilient lives. The result is not bitterness but blessing. The family that learns to turn lemons into lemonade becomes a living testimony that God's grace is sufficient for every sour circumstance.

In the end, sour seasons do not define a family. They refine it. The lemon teaches that even the sharpest experiences can be transformed by love and purpose. With prayer as the sweetener and patience as the water, the sour seasons of parenting become the very ingredients of joy. When guided by God, the once-bitter moments mature into the beautiful taste of resilience.

Reflection Questions

1. When my child faces a "sour season," do I react in frustration or respond in faith?

2. What might God be cleansing or strengthening in my family through this difficult phase?

3. How do I balance discipline and grace so that correction purifies but does not wound?

4. In what ways have past challenges made me or my child stronger, wiser, or more compassionate?

5. What practices can I put in place to remind myself that every sour season has a divine purpose?

FRUIT OF THE WOMB

A Prayer of Blessing

Heavenly Father,

Thank You for the wisdom You hide in life's lemons. When seasons turn sour, teach me to see Your hand at work. Give me patience when I am weary, clarity when I am confused, and tenderness when my words could wound. Help me to guide my children through their difficult moments with grace and strength.

May the sour seasons in our home become times of cleansing and growth. Transform what is bitter into a blessing, what is painful into a purpose, and what feels sharp into something that refreshes. Let our family be a testimony that endurance produces character, and character produces hope.

Lord, remind me that every moment of discipline, every tear of frustration, and every act of perseverance is shaping resilience for tomorrow. As lemons preserve and purify, may Your Spirit preserve our hearts and purify our love. We trust you to bring sweetness from every sour season. In Jesus' name, Amen.

FRUIT OF THE WOMB

Practical Family Activity – "Lemonade from Lemons"

Step 1 – Taste the Sour:

Bring a few lemons to the table. Slice one and have each family member taste it. Let everyone react, laugh at the faces, describe the flavor, and feel the sharpness. Then say together, "This is how life can feel sometimes, sour, sharp, and surprising."

Step 2 – Mix the Sweetness:

Add water and sugar, stirring as a family. As you mix, explain, "God doesn't remove the sour things in life. He teaches us how to mix them with His love and patience until they become something beautiful."

Step 3 – Share the Lessons:

Invite each person to recall a recent "sour" moment, maybe a mistake, conflict, or disappointment. Discuss what each person learned or how they grew. Parents can share too; vulnerability models maturity.

Step 4 – Drink and Declare:

Pour the lemonade, raise the glasses, and declare together:

"God turns our sour seasons into sweetness. We will not waste our lemons. We will grow from them."

Step 5 – Pray Together:

Close in prayer, thanking God for His transforming grace and asking Him to make every sour moment a source of strength and joy.

CHAPTER 12

THE PEAR: BALANCE AND WHOLENESS

The pear is a fruit of quiet grace. It lacks the vivid crown of the pineapple or the dramatic sharpness of the lemon, yet its beauty lies in its simplicity. The pear does not demand attention; it offers it gently, smooth to the eye, soft to the touch, sweet to the taste, and satisfying to the body. Its balance of sweetness and substance makes it both comforting and nourishing. The pear teaches us that harmony, not excess, is the secret to wholeness.

Children, like pears, flourish best when their lives are nurtured in balance. The goal of parenting is not to produce extremes, not the sweetest, toughest, smartest, or most disciplined child, but a whole child. God's design is not perfection in one area and poverty in another, but maturity that integrates every part of the person. Luke 2:52 gives us the divine blueprint: "And Jesus grew in wisdom and stature, and in favor with God and man." Even the Son of God, who was perfect in spirit, chose to mature in balance, intellectually (wisdom), physically (stature), spiritually (favor with God), and socially (favor with man).

That single verse contains the secret to holistic parenting. Raising a balanced child means helping them grow not only in skill and strength but in heart and soul. Too often, parents chase measurable results such as grades, sports achievements, manners, or religious behavior while neglecting unseen dimensions like peace, curiosity, and empathy. Yet true fruitfulness cannot come from imbalance. The pear, perfectly shaped and proportioned, reminds us that beauty and nourishment are inseparable. A life that looks whole but is emotionally or spiritually undernourished cannot endure.

Balance does not happen naturally; it must be cultivated. A pear does not ripen overnight. It matures slowly, changing from green to gold under the right conditions of light, warmth, and time. Parenting is the same, a process of patient nurturing where every area of a child's life is given the opportunity to ripen. If rushed, the fruit bruises. If ignored, it spoils. If overexposed, it hardens before its time. The art of raising balanced children is, therefore, the art of patience, knowing when to wait, when to guide, and when to let God's grace ripen what He planted.

The pear's gentleness also reveals something about God's own nature. He does not overwhelm us with sweetness nor crush us with strength. His dealings with His children are always balanced, firm yet kind, truthful yet merciful, corrective yet compassionate. Psalm 85:10 describes this divine harmony beautifully: "Mercy and truth are met together; righteousness and peace have kissed each other." That is the rhythm of godly parenting, the ability to blend firmness with tenderness, to train while still embracing, to discipline while still delighting.

Parents who live in extremes, all strictness and no softness or all indulgence and no structure, will eventually see imbalance mirrored in their children. But when the home reflects God's balance, children grow confident and whole. They learn that strength is safe, that love has boundaries, and that obedience brings joy.

The pear's moderate sweetness also teaches restraint. Its taste is pleasant but not overpowering. Children, too, need a balance between pleasure and purpose. A generation raised only on comfort will lack endurance, while a generation raised only on correction will lack joy. Wholeness requires both. Ecclesiastes 3:11 declares, "He has made everything beautiful in its time." Parents who nurture balance understand timing, when to let laughter fill the home and when to quiet hearts for reflection, when to challenge and when to comfort.

Balance is not sameness. It does not erase individuality. Just as each pear has its unique shade and curve, each child has a distinct temperament and calling. One may ripen early, another slowly. One may shine in intellect, another in compassion. God delights in diversity, not uniformity. Parents who understand balance celebrate differences without comparison. They know that harmony in the family does not come from everyone being identical but from each one being developed according to their God-given design.

True balance, then, is spiritual alignment. It is the parents' daily act of tuning their hearts to God so that their words, tone, and priorities echo His. Like the careful pruning of a tree, balance requires removing what grows too wildly, an overemphasis on performance, for instance, while nurturing what has been neglected, such as joy, prayer, or rest. A balanced parent raises balanced children.

Building the Shape of Wholeness

The pear's shape is distinctive, wide at the base and narrowing gracefully toward the top. Its form is a living parable of balanced growth. The wide base represents foundation, love, security, and faith, while the narrowing top points toward maturity, purpose, and destiny. Parents who build a strong base make it possible for their children to grow upward without collapse.

Many homes struggle not because children refuse to grow but because their foundations are too narrow. They are pushed upward into achievement, visibility, or independence before being rooted in identity. Like a pear that ripens unevenly, they appear mature in some areas but remain fragile in others. Wholeness begins at the base, in belonging, discipline, and spiritual grounding.

1. Love and Belonging – The Base of Security

Children must first know they are loved unconditionally. Before rules, chores, or lessons, the heart must be anchored in acceptance. A child's sense of belonging is the soil in which every other virtue grows. 1 John 4:19 reminds us, "We love because he first loved us." When children are secure in love, correction does not crush them, and failure does not define them.

Parents sometimes confuse love with indulgence. Love does not mean saying yes to everything; it means being present through everything. It means setting boundaries from affection, not anger. It means listening without judgment and disciplining without rejection. A home filled with this kind of love becomes fertile ground for emotional stability.

2. Discipline and Guidance – The Spine of Stability

The second layer of balance is discipline. Without structure, love becomes sentimentality. Proverbs 29:17 teaches, "Discipline your children, and they will give you peace; they will bring you the delights you desire." Discipline, properly applied, is the spine that keeps the body upright. It helps children connect actions with consequences and freedom with responsibility.

But discipline must never be separated from relationship. The goal is not control but character. Parents should remember that God disciplines His children not to punish but to shape them. Hebrews 12:10 says, "God disciplines us for our good, so that we may share in his holiness." When children understand that correction flows from love, they learn respect without resentment.

3. Faith and Identity – The Root of Direction

The pear's sweetness draws from deep roots, and in the same way, a child's wholeness is sustained by spiritual grounding. In a world where identities shift like sand, faith anchors the soul. Teaching children who they are in Christ protects them from insecurity and confusion. Psalm 127:3 reminds us, "Children are a heritage from the Lord, offspring a reward from him."

FRUIT OF THE WOMB

Parents who instill faith early are planting roots that withstand drought. Daily prayer, reading Scripture together, and conversations about God's presence make spirituality tangible. This is not mere religion but relational discipleship, helping children see that God cares about their schoolwork, their friendships, and their fears.

When these three, love, discipline, and faith, form the base, a child's growth upward becomes steady. Their emotional, intellectual, and social development builds on a strong foundation. Like a well-shaped pear, their life stands firm and balanced, capable of weathering both success and struggle.

The pear also reminds us that wholeness is nourishing, not ornamental. Its sweetness satisfies, but its fiber strengthens. Children raised in wholeness not only charm others with personality, but they also sustain others with integrity. They are emotionally intelligent, spiritually grounded, and socially wise. The world needs such balanced individuals, people who can think clearly, feel deeply, and act justly.

But the imbalance threatens this harmony. A pear misshapen by neglect or overgrowth loses its appeal and strength. Likewise, when parents overemphasize one dimension of growth, such as academics without empathy or faith without wisdom, children become lopsided. Imbalance breeds fragility. A child who excels in studies but lacks compassion may become proud. Another who is deeply spiritual but undisciplined may struggle to apply faith practically. God's design is symmetry, the harmony of multiple strengths held together by humility.

Jesus' life again provides the model. He grew intellectually ("in wisdom") by engaging teachers and asking questions. He grew physically ("in stature") by laboring in His earthly father's workshop. He grew spiritually ("in favor with God") through prayer and obedience. He grew socially ("in favor with man") through service, empathy, and relationships. No aspect was neglected; every layer was integrated. His balance prepared Him for the purpose.

Parents who follow that model raise children who reflect Christ's harmony. They do not chase comparison or perfection but maturity, a wholeness that can handle the weight of destiny. Like the pear, whose strength lies in quiet symmetry, balanced children stand firm without shouting for attention. Their presence refreshes; their lives bear fruit that nourishes others.

Wholeness, then, is not a destination but a daily alignment. It is the parents' ongoing prayer: "Lord, make me balanced so I can raise balanced children." When we model calm instead of chaos, grace instead of pressure, and faith instead of fear, we give our children something priceless: the pattern of peace.

FRUIT OF THE WOMB

Living and Leaving a Legacy of Balance

The beauty of the pear is not only in how it looks or tastes, but in what it represents, a harmony that lasts beyond its own season. Balance, once cultivated, becomes legacy. A tree that bears balanced fruit can nourish others long after the harvest. In the same way, a parent who learns to live with balance does more than raise a good child; they model a way of life that blesses generations.

Children not only inherit their parents' words; they absorb their rhythms. They watch how adults handle joy and disappointment, success and failure, pressure and rest. They notice when love is given freely and when peace rules the atmosphere of the home. A child learns balance not merely through lectures but through observation. When parents respond to stress with prayer instead of panic, forgive instead of retaliate, and pause to listen instead of rushing to correct, they are quietly teaching their children how to live whole.

The pear ripens best when left to mature naturally. Forced ripening produces artificial sweetness that fades quickly. So, it is with children. The pressure to achieve, perform, or appear perfect can create emotional distortion. Parents must allow growth to occur at God's pace, not societies. The journey of childhood is not a race but a ripening. When the process is honored, character develops as beautifully as flavor in fruit left to mature under the patient sun.

Balance is sustained by presence. A pear tree thrives where it is planted, drawing nourishment from steady soil and regular rain. Children thrive when parents are present, not just physically but emotionally and spiritually. Presence communicates worth. It tells a child, *"You matter enough for me to stop and see you."* In a world of constant distraction, presence is sacred. The ministry of attention is one of the most healing gifts a parent can offer. It says more than any lecture: *"I am here, and I delight in you."*

A balanced home does not mean a perfect home. It means a peaceful one. Peace is not the absence of noise but the presence of order. When love guides decisions, when communication is gentle, and when laughter and prayer mingle freely, the atmosphere itself becomes nurturing. Children raised in such environments grow to value harmony. They instinctively resist chaos because they have known calm.

Balance also means embracing seasons. A pear tree does not bear fruit all year long; it has times of budding, flowering, fruiting, and resting. Parents, too, must recognize the seasons of their children's development. There are years of instruction when discipline is strong, years of exploration when curiosity must be encouraged, and years of transition when trust becomes the bridge between childhood and adulthood. To insist that every season produce the same result is to miss God's rhythm. Wise parents flow with it, pruning when necessary, watering with encouragement, and waiting patiently when growth seems slow.

Spiritual balance is the unseen strength beneath every other kind. Without it, emotional, intellectual, and social growth can lose direction. Children who know God personally, not merely through sermons but through daily conversation, prayer, and example, develop an inner compass that steadies them when life pulls in opposite directions. Teaching them to seek God in both triumph and trial grounds their souls. They learn that success without gratitude leads to pride, and suffering without faith leads to despair. But when both are viewed through the lens of divine purpose, life itself becomes balanced.

Wholeness, then, is not simply about doing well in all areas; it is about living *integrated*, where the spiritual, emotional, and practical parts of life all feed each other. When a child learns that prayer can coexist with play, that discipline can walk hand in hand with joy, and that learning can be as sacred as worship, they begin to live the kind of balance Jesus modeled.

FRUIT OF THE WOMB

The greatest expression of balance is love expressed through wisdom. Love without wisdom spoils; wisdom without love wounds. But love guided by wisdom nurtures growth without distortion. It helps children navigate freedom without rebellion, correction without shame, and faith without fear. Parents who practice this balance are mirrors of the divine, reflecting God's steadiness in a world of extremes.

As children mature, they begin to mirror back what they have absorbed. A young adult who has seen calm through crises learns to be unshaken by difficulty. One who has watched forgiveness modeled grows merciful. One who has been prayed for consistently begins to pray instinctively. Like a pear tree producing fruit after its kind, balanced parenting reproduces balanced adulthood.

This legacy extends far beyond one generation. The fruit of balanced parenting ripples outward into how children treat others, raise their own families, handle conflict, and contribute to their communities. A single life lived in balance can quietly reform a lineage. *"A generous person will prosper; whoever refreshes others will be refreshed"* (Proverbs 11:25). Parents who live generously with time, grace, and patience refresh their children, who in turn refresh others.

The pear also whispers a quieter truth, that balance is sustained through pruning. Even the healthiest trees must occasionally lose branches to bear better fruit. Parents, too, must prune distractions, unhealthy expectations, and even personal pride to maintain equilibrium. This pruning may be uncomfortable, but it keeps the soul fruitful. *"Every branch that bears fruit, He prunes so that it will be even more fruitful"* (John 15:2). The pruning of imbalance is the preservation of peace.

In the end, balance is not just what we give our children but what we become for them. When a child sees a parent live with centered joy, steady faith, and quiet strength, they are seeing the Gospel in motion. It teaches them that the life of faith is not chaotic striving but ordered grace. And that lesson, once learned, can sustain them for a lifetime.

FRUIT OF THE WOMB

Reflection Questions

1. In what areas of my child's growth do I notice imbalance, and how might I restore harmony without resorting to extremes?

2. Do I model a balanced life in front of my child, or do I allow work, stress, or emotion to overshadow peace?

3. How can I create an atmosphere at home where both laughter and correction coexist with grace?

4. What daily habits, prayer, meals, and conversations can help our family remain spiritually and emotionally centered?

5. How can I remind my child, through my actions, that maturity takes time and balance is God's design for growth?

FRUIT OF THE WOMB

A Prayer of Blessing

Heavenly Father, you are the God of perfect balance, strong yet gentle, just yet merciful. Thank You for creating my child with depth and dimension, for giving them a mind to think, a heart to feel, a body to grow, and a spirit to connect with You. Teach me to nurture each part in harmony. Guard me from extremes that wound, and guide me toward the steady wisdom that heals. Let peace govern our home, patience fill our conversations, and joy season our days. May my child, like a pear ripened in the sun, grow into wholeness, balanced in wisdom, stature, and favor with You and with others. *In Jesus' name, Amen.*

Practical Family Activity: "Pear of Balance"

Gather as a family and share fresh pears together. As each person takes a slice, talk about the qualities of the fruit, its firmness, sweetness, and gentle refreshment. Let this simple act become a living illustration. Remind everyone that, like the pear, balance makes life beautiful. Invite each family member to reflect aloud: in what area do they feel strong, and in what area do they need more growth? Discuss how even Jesus grew in four ways: in wisdom, stature, favor with God, and favor with man.

FRUIT OF THE WOMB

End by holding hands in prayer, asking God to shape your family into one of balance, emotionally steady, spiritually anchored, intellectually curious, socially compassionate, and physically healthy. Encourage everyone to commit to one small act of balance for the week, perhaps more rest, more listening, more prayer, or more laughter. As you do, remember that the goal is not perfection but peace. Just as the pear nourishes body and soul with quiet sweetness, may your home become a place where balance ripens naturally under the light of God's love.

CONCLUSION

THE HARVEST – RAISING A FRUITFUL GENERATION

Parenting is cultivation, a sacred partnership between divine intention and human stewardship. Throughout this book, we have explored how children resemble fruit, unique in form, flavor, and fragrance, yet all designed to nourish and delight. Apples, bananas, grapes, pineapples, oranges, strawberries, coconuts, lemons, and pears have each shown us something vital about raising a child in wisdom and grace. Like fruit, children mature best in healthy soil, under patient care, and within an environment that balances nourishment and pruning. To parent is to tend the orchard of God.

Just as a farmer labor with hope, waiting for the unseen seed to push through the soil, so parents pour out love, discipline, and faith long before the results are visible. *Psalm 127:3 declares, "Children are a heritage from the Lord, offspring a reward from him."* This heritage demands intentional tending. Growth does not occur by accident; it is the result of consistent care and the slow accumulation of daily faithfulness. Each bedtime prayer, gentle correction, and word of encouragement becomes a drop of water upon the tender roots of a child's soul.

FRUIT OF THE WOMB

Parenting, at its core, is about preparing for harvest. No farmer plants seed merely for the sake of leaves or blossoms; the goal is fruit that nourishes, multiplies, and sustains life. In the same way, the aim of raising children is not simply to produce good behavior or worldly success but to nurture fruitfulness, character that glorifies God and blesses others. Fruitful children become adults who embody integrity, compassion, and calling. They refresh weary souls, bring sweetness to bitter spaces, and multiply goodness in every sphere they touch. Their maturity is not measured by perfection but by purpose. Their fruit reveals their roots.

Jesus expressed this truth clearly when He said, "This is to my Father's glory, that you bear much fruit, showing yourselves to be my disciples" (John 15:8). Parenting fulfills its mission not when children merely survive or achieve, but when they become bearers of fruit that reflects their divine source. Our joy as parents is found in seeing the Spirit's fruit, love, joy, peace, patience, kindness, goodness, faithfulness, gentleness, and self-control ripen in our children's lives.

One of the wonders of fruit is that it carries within it the seed for more fruit. Every apple holds an orchard in potential. Every grape contains a vineyard in miniature. What we nurture in our children today becomes the foundation for future generations. Children are not only the fruit of our present labor; they are the seedbed of

FRUIT OF THE WOMB

tomorrow's harvest. A godly home today can influence families, communities, and even nations tomorrow. Our children's faith, values, and example will outlive us and shape the moral and spiritual landscape of generations yet to come.

Psalm 128:3–4 offers this beautiful vision: "Your children will be like olive shoots around your table. Yes, this will be the blessing for the man who fears the Lord." When we raise our children in reverence and righteousness, we are planting olive trees whose roots will outlast our own lifetimes. The harvest of one family can transform the soil of an entire society.

But no harvest comes without seasons. The farmer knows the rhythm of the earth, the waiting of winter, the promise of spring, the work of summer, and the joy of autumn. So it is with parenting. There are seasons of laughter, where every word and gesture feels effortless. There are seasons of frustration, where discipline feels endless and results are invisible. There are seasons of pruning, when hard choices must be made to preserve character over comfort. And there are seasons of celebration, when we see glimpses of the fruit we have prayed for.

Ecclesiastes 3:1 reminds us, "To everything there is a season, and a time for every purpose under heaven." Wise parents learn to recognize these times, not resenting them but embracing them as part of the divine cycle. Growth cannot be rushed. Some roots strengthen in silence. Some fruit ripens only in heat. Faithful parenting requires patience, the willingness to believe that even when you cannot see progress, God is still at work beneath the surface.

The beauty of parenting also lies in diversity. Walk through an orchard and you will see it, each tree with its own shape, rhythm, and kind of fruit. No two fruits are identical, yet each fulfills a unique role in creation. In the same way, children differ in temperament, talent, and pace. One child may be bold and adventurous, another reflective and gentle. One thrives on structure, another blooms through creativity. To parent well is to discern rather than compare, to cultivate rather than control. Each child is a divine original.

Scripture teaches that the body of Christ has many parts, each vital to the whole (*1 Corinthians 12*). God's orchard is no different. He plants a variety intentionally. The sweetness of one life complements the tartness of another. As parents, our call is not to shape our children into copies of ourselves, but to help them discover who God made them to be. A wise gardener does not scold a lemon for being sour or a strawberry for being soft; they tend each according to its kind. Likewise, love must be tailored, not standardized.

FRUIT OF THE WOMB

Of course, cultivation can be tiring work. Parenting requires long hours and longer faith. There are days when the soil feels hard, the sun too hot, and the harvest too far away. Yet even then, God's Word whispers encouragement: *"Let us not become weary in doing good, for at the proper time we will reap a harvest if we do not give up" (Galatians 6:9)*. The farmer's joy is not just in the fruit but in the journey, in the memory of every sunrise that met faithful hands still tending the field.

One day, those who have labored in love will taste the reward. The child once cradled in uncertainty will stand firm in faith. The prayers whispered in tears will return as testimonies of grace. The sacrifices that seemed unnoticed will be crowned with gratitude and legacy. That is the parent's reward, the quiet satisfaction of seeing fruit where once there was only seed, of realizing that every act of faithfulness mattered.

And so, as we conclude this journey, the message is clear: parenting is holy cultivation. Children are not accidents of biology but gifts of divinity. They are living orchards, requiring care, discipline, and light. Parents are not passive observers but gardeners in God's kingdom, called to plant truth, water faith, prune pride, and harvest joy. The work is sacred because the outcome is eternal. Every word of affirmation, every prayer spoken in secret, and every consistent act of love are seeds that heaven will honor.

FRUIT OF THE WOMB

The ultimate goal is not simply to raise good families but to shape a fruitful generation, sons and daughters who glorify God, bless others, and reproduce righteousness. Parenting is one of the highest forms of ministry. Each meal shared, each hug offered, and each conversation infused with grace becomes part of a divine story of cultivation that stretches beyond our lifetime. The orchard we tend today will nourish a world we may never see.

Let us therefore parent with vision, eyes lifted beyond the immediate mess of the moment toward the eternal harvest to come. For the same God who began the good work in our children will be faithful to complete it. And when we finally see the fruit of that labor, when our children stand firm in faith, walking in wisdom, and raising their own children in love, we will know that every seed sown in prayer was worth the wait.

Reflection Questions for Parents

1. Looking back over the "fruits" in this book, which one most reflects my child's current season of growth?

2. Which fruit's lesson challenges me most as a parent: sweetness, resilience, balance, or tenderness?

3. How have I been faithful in cultivating my children's growth, and where do I need God's help to be more intentional?

4. What harvest do I desire in my children's future, not just in achievement but in faith, character, and legacy?

5. Am I parenting with a generational vision, seeing my children not only as fruit but also as seed for the future?

FRUIT OF THE WOMB

Final Prayer of Blessing

Lord of the Harvest,

Thank you for entrusting children to our care. Teach us to be faithful gardeners in Your orchard. Help us to see their sweetness, endure their sour seasons, protect their tenderness, and guide them into balance. May our homes be places of light, where Your Word takes root deeply and Your love grows freely.

Let our children flourish like trees planted by rivers of living water, fruitful in every season, unshaken by the winds of the world. May they grow in wisdom, in stature, and in favor with You and with people. Grant us patience to labor in faith and joy to reap in time. We trust that the seeds of love we plant will yield a harvest of righteousness and peace.

In Jesus' name, Amen.

FRUIT OF THE WOMB

Practical Family Activity: "Harvest Celebration"

1. Gather a basket of assorted fruits such as apples, grapes, pears, bananas, lemons, and others.

2. As a family, hold each fruit and recall the lesson it represents: sweetness, strength, resilience, tenderness, balance, or wholeness.

3. Parents take turns affirming each child by saying, *"You are like this fruit because..."* and speak blessings over them.

4. Pray together, thanking God for His orchard of children and asking Him to bring forth a harvest of faith and fruitfulness.

5. Share the fruit together in joy as a symbolic family harvest meal, celebrating the love and growth within your home.

FRUIT OF THE WOMB

www.ingramcontent.com/pod-product-compliance
Lightning Source LLC
Chambersburg PA
CBHW071202160426

43196CB00011B/2162